FISH
and be
DAMNED

or
The Night Crawler's Companion

Written and Illustrated by
LAWRENCE LARIAR

HAMMOND, HAMMOND & COMPANY, LONDON

PRINTED IN GREAT BRITAIN
FOR HAMMOND, HAMMOND AND CO. LTD., 87 GOWER STREET, LONDON, W.C.1,
BY LOWE AND BRYDONE (PRINTERS) LTD., LONDON, N.W.10

WHY FISH ARE SMARTER THAN ANYBODY

The average fisherman is pretty sure he's much smarter than the average fish. He is so scornful of fish that he uses them as a symbol of stupidity. When a man wants to ridicule another man, he will invariably call him: "A poor fish." Any psychiatrist will tell you that this is because of an actual feeling of inferiority on the part of the man.

Deep down in his heart, he knows that most fish are a hell of a lot smarter than he is. That's why it costs him $6.78 in bait and tackle to land one porgy, worth only 17 cents on the open fish market.

You never hear one fish calling another fish: "A poor man." This comes about because fish know when to keep their mouths shut. They've been on earth for approximately 8,657,980 years, a long time before the first human arrived. During that time, they learned the rules for survival. They just mind their own business, avoid worry, eat simple foods and keep on laying eggs.

Man, on the other hand, worked hard to develop his cranium. And where did it get him? He used his brain to create modern conveniences, make lots of money and then buy his wife a mink coat. Any half-wit herring will tell you this is just plain stupidity. You never saw a female herring sporting a mink wrap, did you?

The daily habits of fish prove them superior to man in almost every way. Take sleeping, for instance. After a night out with the boys, the male mackerel slides behind a convenient rock and lays there until breakfast time. He sleeps with his eyes open. When it's time for his morning meal, he's full of pep, despite the fact he hasn't closed his eyes all night. No man alive could operate that way. Even with 10 Bromos!

Average Herring at 7 A.M.   **Average Man at 7 A.M.**

Ichthyologists have not yet discovered a fish stupid enough to talk to anybody. By keeping his trap shut, even the dumbest stickleback looks like an intellectual to his associates. Talking, for most fish, is a waste of time. An amorous albacore will flip his fin at a passing female and sell her the idea without opening his yap. And he never gets his face slapped that way.

The fact that fish know exactly what to eat proves how smart they are.

You don't have to write a special diet for a smelt. Every female smelt is svelte because she knows enough to limit her diet to plankton, aquatic hors-d'oeuvres and small bits of sea weed. You'll never catch her nibbling on candy bars at odd hours.

The sex life of the fish is a shining example of simplicity and intelligence. Adolescent cods rarely have to run back to mamma to discuss the facts of life. They are taught from early childhood that a healthy male cod must preserve his virility by never smoking, drinking, or playing cod games. Nor does he hang around the corner drug store whistling at girls. All he does is swim around for a few hours until he finds a mate. Then he simply coddles her.

The female cod soon eggs him on, but he is allowed to go out with the boys while she mothers the brood. A fairly average mamma cod can produce a few billion babies successfully. And she isn't half trying.

The mother cod doesn't spoil her offspring. They are allowed to roam free with the bunch, turn up their noses at spinach and mingle with

Average female cod with 1,768,654   Average female human with one (1)
babies.   baby.

friends of their own choosing. Despite this freedom from mamma's apron strings, most of her kids grow up to be strong, active, healthy codfish cakes.

The fact that Mrs. Cod can accomplish this feat at least once a season is not at all startling to other cods. You never heard of a mother cod needing a maid, either.

Most fishermen think fish are stupid because they get caught on baited hooks. This has nothing at all to do with the fish's intelligence. If a speckled trout had hands, he'd pick the bait off the hook and beat it. Any fisherman who doubts this should pause to remember this fact: nine out of ten speckled trout can remove your bait *with no hands!*

But what happens when a clever fish decides to catch himself a man? You won't find a hungry shark bothering to bait a hook with a ham sandwich when he wants to dine on a human being. The shark just moves in fast and grabs his man. By using the direct approach, he proves his basic intelligence. And he saves a hell of a lot of money on special bait, lures and sinkers.

Even very young fish can outthink any human child on the same age level. Small fry and fingerlings never resent going to school. Statistics show that the junior herring stays in schools all his life. This eliminates such things as child psychologists, vocational guidance counsellors, and juvenile delinquent herrings.

The teen-age tuna is polite and placid and rarely beset by emotional problems. The adolescent angel fish is independent, mature and able to stay clear of vagrant devil fishes. The youthful flounder rarely flounders.

And no scientist has yet discovered a maladjusted mackerel.

THE HERRING

Herrings really leave me cold,
They're neither brazen, brave nor bold,
But born to swim in mob or school
And live their lives by rote and rule.
Yet death's supreme finality
Hands herrings personality,
For once deceased, they gain a flavor
That every gourmet seems to savor.
Emerging as a toothsome dream
When buried under sour cream.

THE CARE AND PREVENTION OF
WOMEN NIMRODS

The other day, whilst cleaning out the moths from my tackle box, I ran cross a covey of letters sent to me while I was Editor in Chief of the *Fisherman's Fortnightly Fly*, a sporting journal that expired shortly after the Boxer Rebellion. In those days my mailbox was always stuffed with *billets-doux* from worried anglers the world over. They would post their problems to me and make no move until I replied in my columns. As a result of this attitude, some of them are still standing motionless in various parts of the world.

The following three epistles are typical examples of the age-old problem of all red-blooded nimrods. And current reports reveal the same symptoms among even the anaemic nimrods:

"Send me the best rig for jigging minnows," asked Calvin J. Cooledge. "My wife refuses to fish for any larger fish."

"My good wife will only go trolling for tripe on tramp trawlers," yammered Walt Dismal, the great Hollywood joy boy producer. "How can I convince her to stay home where she belongs?"

"Is it true that arsenic, in small doses, can kill a woman?" inquired a worried character named Jack Deripper. " My wife doesn't seem to respond."

See what I mean? A further study of Cooledge, Dismal and Deripper revealed that all three sportsmen had long since paid the supreme penalty in the electric chair for murdering their mates. Such a practice, while eliminating the source of annoyance immediately, has permanent ill effects on a man's fishing habits. Cooledge, Dismal and Deripper evidenced symptoms of bad manners and worse timing. Any fool could have told them that women have been going in for masculine sports ever since they earned the right to vote for the wrong candidate. Today, millions of females fancy themselves expert anglers, grabbing men's rods and rushing off to stream and brook.

"My wife has pinched my rod again!" is the wail of the married nimrod heard from Bangor to Butte. "What can I do to keep her away from my equipment? What can I do to fish alone again?"

The answer to this mournful plea must come from the mouth of the immortal Henry Wadsworth Longfinny, who said: "If you can't lick 'em, pals — join 'em!" This advice, though useless for all men who prefer to lick their wives, may prove helpful to those who happen to be sissies. For all others, the following suggestions, compiled after years of personal research, may help you over the rough spots:

1: THE "DOWN THE NOSE" OR BELITTLING ATTACK

When your frau expresses the desire to join you fishing, you may find yourself overcome by a variety of emotions. Some men rear back on their haunches, snarl, yell, and show their bile. Other men find their throats going dry, turn pale and jittery, or sag at the knees. Still others froth at the mouth and simply explode.

This type of behavior will get you nowhere. The best method for handling your little woman's yen for rod and reel requires will power, self-control and a good strong stomach. It is useless to open your emotional valves at such a time. Instead, simply grin at your mate condescendingly, in the manner of a cat smiling at a canary. Chuckle a bit. After that, the scenario might go this way:

YOU: *(still smiling)* "Did you say you wanted to go fishing, Zelda?"
ZELDA: *(firmly)* "You heard me, Horace. And wipe that stupid smirk
            off your face."

YOU: "I'm not smirking, dear. I'm happy you've decided to fish with me. But why the sudden interest?"

ZELDA: "I think I'll enjoy the sport, that's why."

YOU: "I hope you're right, Zelda. But fishing's such a sloppy sport, at best."

ZELDA: "I like sloppy sports. I married you, didn't I?"

YOU: *(still pleasant)* "And fishing's disgusting, in a way. Take worms, for instance —"

ZELDA: "Like I said before, I can get along with worms. We've been married for twelve years, haven't we?"

YOU: *(unabashed by the sarcasm)* "The fact is that women just don't do well at fishing, Zelda."

ZELDA: *(brightly)* "Don't make me laugh, stupid. The records show that Mrs. H. A. Bradley, Jr., caught the world's record Black Drum at Cape Charles, Virginia on May 6th, 1950. Mrs. Earl Small broke the world's record when she caught a White Perch weighing 4 pounds and 12 ounces in 1949. Mrs. Lee Hallberg pulled in the record Silver Salmon, a puny 31 pounder. And Mrs. I. L. Hayes managed to bring in a 63 pound lake trout with her lily white hands back in 1930."

YOU: *(doubtfully)* "Sez who?"

ZELDA: "Sez the latest *World Almanac*. Had enough?"

YOU: *(weakly)* "Glgggggzsssh ————"

(CURTAIN)

As the curtain descends we find our hero walking slowly toward the family car wondering how he can ever face his fishing companions again. He has been trapped, hoodwinked and hoisted by his own petard. Yet, all hope is not lost. He may still avail himself of the following methods:

2: THE EMOTIONAL OR PRE-DEPARTURE ATTACK

Once a woman has made up her mind to knit a doily, make a lamb stew or go fishing, only great tact and patience can change her mind. Women are blessed with stubborn, arbitrary dispositions, aided and abetted by good muscles. If your wife suddenly announces that she will join you for tomorrow's fishing, accept her decision with a quiet smile.

Just before dinner is the best time to spoil her appetite for the sport. The time is just right for carrying a few dozen bloodworms into the kitchen. Explain that you are about to demonstrate the correct way for baiting a hook. Begin to thread the fattest bloodworm you can find on the thinnest hook. The sight of this gory mess may go a long way toward ruining your wife's dinner. Some wives are subject to violent fits of retching by the sight of bloodworms. However, if she doesn't react after the third worm, abandon the idea. You may get pretty nauseated, yourself.

3: THE PURPOSEFUL DETOUR OR DELAYING TACTIC

Let us assume that your wife has survived Method Number 2 and simply adores dripping bloodworms. Your next strategy simply requires a minor knowledge of automobile engines. Before leaving in the car, open the petcock under the radiator. Allow a few gallons of water to drain off. Now you are ready to depart for the lake.

Make sure to take the longest way to your destination, a road that leads on a wide detour, off the beaten track. When the engine begins to boil and steam, stop the car and make puzzled, hopeless gestures over the motor. Since you are now at least five miles from the last isolated gas station, suggest that she remain in the car while you go for a mechanic. Now walk slowly down the road. Correct pacing should consume half a day's time before car is fixed for further use.

(Note: Dire tragedies have resulted when such plans are tried on women of the wrong type. If your wife is an ex-war-plant worker, or mechanically inclined, do not attempt to use this strategy. Remember, she knows how to use a Stillson Wrench!)

4: THE GREEN FLY OR GNATS TO YOU METHOD

If your wife has survived the foregoing schemes, you have but one last tactic left to you. Steer a direct course for the most uncomfortable spot you've ever found for fishing.

In and around your favorite lake, pond, stream or brook, there is always one location abounding in gnats, mosquitoes, bees, wasps or hornets. For best results, select the gnat area. These little insects can be relied on for steady, unremitting annoyance. In salt water, steer your course for that low spot near the reeds where the green flies hang out.

A few hundred stings on legs, arms and other vulnerable sections of the anatomy will discourage even the most hardy lady nimrod. While recuperating from your own bites, make no complaints. You may be invalided for a month or so, but the next time you go fishing, you'll probably go alone.

Unless your wife isn't bothered by insects.

THE TUNA

Despite his great and fighting heart,
I've never thought the tuna smart.
Despite his strength and staying powers,
Despite the fact he'll tug for hours,
Despite his rushing, savage drive
To lose your hook and stay alive,
Despite the compliments we pay him
Ere we drag him close and slay him,
The point is that he took the bait
As stupidly as cod or skate.
His intellect is hardly valid —
For he winds up as tuna salad!

SALT OR FRESH?

The world of fishing is divided into two types of enthusiasts: The Fresh-water (or *aqua pura*) nimrod, and: The Salt-water (or *saline*) breed. These two groups of sportsmen are continually found sneering at each other, throwing rocks, or making disgusting noises with tongue and mouth. For centuries this feud has existed, despite all efforts from pulpit, rostrum and Small Claims Courts.

In an effort to throw a small tub of oil upon the troubled waters, I've developed the following comparison chart, specially designed to show both types exactly where they stand:

SALT WATER	FRESH WATER
Availability	
Salt water can be found up and down both coasts of the land, due to the movement of tides, eddies, currents and lots of land to slap up against.	Fresh water is limited to lakes, ponds, streams and rivers, which usually come in narrow slices and exist in remote spots that must be reached by overland hikes, canoes and Indian guides.
Fishability	
Salt water is lousy with fish, many of which prefer to swim close to above-mentioned coastal areas for feeding, browsing, mating and other personal reasons. Most bay and ocean fish are extroverts, willing to bite at anything, even a passing psychiatrist.	The fish in fresh water are usually few and furtive, scattered among tall grass, rocks, mud and other impedimenta. Since fresh-water fish have little company, they develop shy, suspicious natures. This holds them away from other fish, populated areas, and anglers' hooks.

Intimate snapshot of Jones (A) and Murgatroyd (B) caught while discussing such subjects as politics, women, religion, books, sex or movies . . .

Same two characters snapped while having a discussion about fishing. (Jones (A) is a salt water devotee. Murgatroyd (B) will only fish in fresh water.)

Cost

Fishing in the sea is practically free. A reasonably expert salt-water, nimrod can get along with only a drop line, sinker, hook and clam. With this equipment he will usuall come home with at least a crab.

Average cost: $2.98

Fresh-water anglers must carry a small tackle store with them wherever they go. They need: rod, reel, flies, lures, leaders, creel, net, plus expensive pipe and tobacco to complete romantic picture. The return for this investment is often only fresh air and sunshine.

Average cost: $22.75

Methodology

The salt-water fisherman has no respect for the fish's mentality. He simply drops the bait, waits and jerks. He is not at all self-conscious about this silly business since he assumes he came out only to grab fish.

The fresh-water angler insists that every fish has an intellect. He therefore tries to lure, trick, out-maneuver, dupe or seduce his quarry. He casts bait, tugs, pulls, teases, tickles, wheedles and cajoles. Net result: more casting, tugging, pulling, teasing, wheedling, cajoling — and sore muscles.

Honesty

Since all fishermen are seasoned liars, there's no point in making comparisons. Fresh-water anglers tell fresher falsehoods. Salt-water fish stories, too, must be taken with a grain of.

("... Henry always prayed for boys — so he could take them fishing with him ...")

EXTRA! FISHERMAN'S BRAIN EXPOSED FOR THE FIRST TIME!

My recent studies in the Bureau of Fish and Chips have stunned the piscatorial world into a state of near panic. X-ray pictures of 6,000 average fishermen revealed the startling fact that 5,999 of them had fish on their minds at all times.

The lone exception turned out to be a fifteen-year-old lad named Cranston Q. Meeker. Meeker admitted that he likes girls, too.

My sample X-ray diagram, attached, proves to the world exactly how the mind of the run of the millstream fisherman works:

1: THE BAIT LOBE

This section of the upper frontal lobe is the part of the brain reserved for bait alone. Here is where the nimrod stores all thoughts about worms, flies, clams and pork rind. Close examination of this lobe will indicate the predominance of worms. This indicates the angler is thinking of fishing for flounders.

Lack of flounders in Section #2 of the cranium indicates that the nimrod has bought the wrong bait.

2: THE FISH LOBE

Any fool can see that the largest portion of the brain is reserved for consideration of the coming day's catch. This roomy, airy section of the cranium has elastic tissues which allow it to stretch to five times

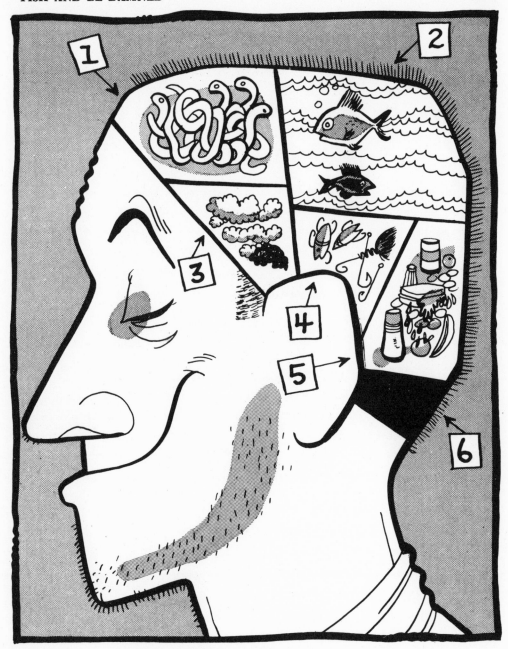

THE FISHERMAN'S CRANIUM

Cross-section view of the average nimrod's brain-basket, as seen through the eye of the X-ray.

its size in the event of an extra large catch. The average fisherman hopes to fill this portion of his brain with a lot of fish at the end of the day.

The existence of so few flounders in this part of his head proves how wrong he can be.

The small bass in the diagram has wandered in by mistake.

3: THE WEATHER LOBE

This tiny department of the cranial cavity is reserved for wishing about the weather. What happens in this section is comparatively unimportant, however, since most fishermen hope for sun and heat, but will go fishing in rain, sleet, blizzard, hurricane and monsoon.

The small *nimbostratus* cloud of black texture that appears in the diagram could mean local showers.

4: THE TACKLE LOBE

This cluttered up segment of the fisherman's brain is devoted exclusively to equipment. Close study will show that the nimrod has brought along lures, rigs, gaffs, line, reels, sinkers, leaders and spoons. Closer examination also reveals that the damned fool forgot to take his flounder hooks. Such a situation must result in (a) a bad migraine, (b) emotional upset, (c) short temper, and (d) no flounders.

5: THE FOOD AND DRINK LOBE

Most scientists agree that this area of the brain is of small importance. It is for this reason we find the lobe loaded with a variety of odd foods.

Notice the stale bread used on the sandwiches.

Note, too, that fruit is soggy and the cookies appear mushy and damp. This comes about because of dripping juice from sardine sandwiches directly above cookies.

The single can of beer will obviously not add much to the day's enjoyment. The pint thermos of coffee is also inadequate. Despite the meager diet, however, the fisherman will return with a bad stomach ache.

This comes about because of the bottle of bourbon one of the boys brought along.

6: THE ALIBI LOBE — OR CHAMBER OF HORRORS

This tiny, darkened chamber on the nimrod's brain will remain a vacuum until he is on the way home. At that time it will flash and sparkle with all kinds of alibis for not catching any fish. Halfway home, the idea chamber will usually produce an inevitable thought.

This will lead to slight detour to nearby fish market.

THE AMBERJACK

The Amberjack lives all his life
Without the nuisance of a wife.
He roams in solitary style,
Nor cares to pause and woo a while.
I've never found him out a-swimmin'
In company of piscine women,
And won't believe he mates, until
I've caught myself an Amberjill.

THE COBIA

Every Cobia
Has a phobia
About the hook
It just took!

A SHORT ESSAY ON LIVE BAIT

What makes a fish bite?

What do fish eat?

Are fish vegetarians?

Can fish actually taste anything?

Do fish shy away from fried foods?

If not, do fish get ulcers?

For years, fishermen have been scratching their heads and asking themselves these important questions. The time is ripe for ending the shilly-shallying methods employed by other experts in the field. There seems to be little doubt that fish go for bait because of one reason. They think it's good to eat.

The personal history of all fish seems to follow a strange pattern. They begin by dining on each other. The only small fish who manage to grow into manhood are those who can avoid the gaping mouths of their elders. Medium-sized fish are eaten by large fish. Large fish are eaten by larger fish.

A twelve inch bass has been known to eat a ten inch perch, lock, stock and dorsal.

After which, the bass suffers no pangs of regret.

And needs no Alka Seltzer, either.

Many fish seem to think that anything moving around in the water is food. Large fish with bad eyesight have been known to gulp down field mice, ducklings, small water snakes and low flying birds, feathers and all. The stomachs of fish have disclosed many strange diets. The Northern

Democratic Pike has been known to eat old Willkie buttons, Confederate medals and even an occasional Southern human finger.

Since so many of our finny friends prefer live bait, it's about time somebody published the lowdown on this little known subject. Every fisherman should be able to go out and gather his own bait. All it takes is a bit of patience, a soupçon of intelligence and a few bucks in your wallet, just in case the following methods fail:

ANGLEWORMS

Let's start out with a long neglected member of the bait family. In the old days, everybody went fishing with angleworms. The zealous nimrod would rise with the dawn, jerk himself into his pants and crawl out behind the barn. He would then dig himself a pailful of these slimy creatures, grab his rod and simply go fishing.

Nowadays it isn't so easy to snare angleworms. This comes about because of the passing of the horse. Since most worms love manure, you'd better find yourself a coöperative animal before beginning your search.

If you live in a horseless area of the country like New York, Detroit or Chicago, either buy yourself a horse, or forget about angleworms.

If you live in heavily populated horse areas, but don't care too much for manure, perhaps we'd better move on to:

Intimate portrait of two angleworms about to announce their engagement.

MINNOWS

There are no less than 150 species of minnows in our fresh waters, and even more in our stale waters. To avoid confusion, I have broken them down into a few common groups. The Latin names are only used here to avoid confusion for Latins:

1. Creek Chub *(Semotilus atromaculatus)*. This is a small chubby looking minnow that has gone up the creek.

2. Red-sided *(Clinostomus Elongatus)*. This is a pinkish type of minnow used by Russian fishermen.

3. Blunt-nosed *(Hyborhynchus Notatus)*. A small minnow with a pug nose and not much personal charm.

4. Mummichog *(Fundulus reteroclitus)*. A common minnow with an uncommon name.

Minnows are the smallest fish alive, but that doesn't make them the easiest to catch. Like small women, they are very mistrustful and shake their tails out of reach when you grab for them. Most fishermen think that minnows are caught easiest when driven into shallow water and then scooped up by hand. This system is all right, provided you're not out alone. You'll need a few dozen friends in the water with you to make this method work. Simply line up and hold hands. Next begin to stomp around in the shallow water to frighten the minnows toward shore.

Some of the minnows will race for the beach. Others will simply stand firm and laugh like hell. You can't honestly blame them.

The simplest way to catch minnows is as follows:

1. Secure a big seine, or net.
2. Fill seine with bread, oatmeal or cracker crumbs.
3. Drop seine into water until it hits the bottom.
4. Wait patiently until you think minnows have rushed in to feed.
5. Now pull up the seine.
6. Take out crabs.
7. Change spot, unless you want to fish for crabs.
8. Start all over again at #1, above.

FROGS

Frogs are specially fine bait for big bass, northern pike and Muskies, but must be fed to these fish while alive and kicking. To keep frogs active and happy, store them in a large bucket filled with moist moss, grass, aquatic plants and other frogs. Lonely frogs sometimes get fits of depression which cause sluggishness and inertia followed by a gradual

pining away. To eliminate such psychiatric symptoms, look for well ad-
justed tadpoles and then raise them through adolescence yourself.

A normal frog will kick and jump, even inside a Musky's belly. A
normal Musky just doesn't give a damn.

To catch your frogs, put on rubbers or overshoes, get yourself a butter-
fly net or an old curtain, and then take a stroll through the nearest marsh.
You will invariably find green frogs in tall green grass. You will also find
the Pickerel Frog in tall green pickerel.

GRASSHOPPERS AND CRICKETS

Any small boy can catch a grasshopper or a cricket.

If you haven't got a small boy around, they're pretty easy to get,
especially if you're married and your wife wants a family.

For married fishermen who don't know how to go about manufactur-
ing small boys, I'd suggest a quick visit to the family doctor who will
lecture briefly on the facts of life. For anglers who have no family doctor
and wish small boys in the family, I'd suggest the purchase of my latest
book: "How Small Boys Are Born," or: "How I Raised Myself from
Failure to Success in the Art of Catching Grasshoppers and Crickets with
Small Boys."

NIGHT CRAWLERS

Contrary to popular belief, these squirmy denizens of the night are
pretty sly, intelligent chaps. Their real name is *Lumbricus terrestris*,
which proves that they existed in ancient Rome and probably fooled
fishermen like Socrates and Julius Caesar, too.

Life size photo of night crawler crawling off into the night.

The only way to catch a night crawler is by way of a flashlight, used in the dead of night where the soil is cool and moist. Expert worm hunters get down on their knees and approach the worm holes with great stealth. Advance upon the worm slowly, lower your hand cautiously and then GRAB! Missed it, didn't you? Now try it again, making sure to stop breathing when about to snatch the worm. If this system fails you are undoubtedly too sluggish for the sport and must go into training to lose a few of those extra pounds.

The best place for catching night crawlers is on a golf course, in the short grass found on greens. If this fails, try the long grass in the rough. If you don't find any worms there, at least you may locate that golf ball you lost last week.

CRAYFISH

Crayfish are also called crawfish, but cray or craw they are dandy bait for trout or bass. Like other crustaceans they shed their outer shells as they grow older. Some fishermen think they are best when caught with their hard shells down during moulting season. Actually, the fish like to nibble on them regardless of the condition of their epidermis. A two inch crayfish looks as good as a porterhouse steak to the fussiest fish in the lake. This proves that fish are cock-eyed.

Some nimrods prefer to hook crayfish through the craw. Others like to hook crawfish through the carapace, or corset. This leads to confusion for the average fisherman, who can't tell the difference between a carapace and a corset unless his wife is wearing it.

HELLGRAMMITES

The Hellgrammite is a youthful corydalis, which means he'd grow up to a sort of dragon fly if fishermen would just leave him alone. Instead, nimrods are continually grubbing around in stream bottoms, under muck and stones, to grab the youthful hellgrammite for trout food. This state of affairs would discourage most other insects from mating and producing progeny. The male corydalis, however, has no moral fibre. Especially when in the presence of a female corydalis. This inevitably leads to more and more hellgrammites.

THE LAMPREY EEL

The very young of this species make very good bait for bass when found no larger than four or five inches. The lamprey has a sucker-like mouth which it uses to cling to the fingers of sucker-like fishermen who come hunting for them.

MICE

This is unusual bait but is worth a try if you happen to have a few handy while fishing. A small mouse is supposed to catch a big brown trout, pike or Musky. This confuses most fishermen who think catfish should grab them.

To put a mouse on your hook requires patience, courage and a heart of ice. Warm-hearted nimrods had better stick to worms and grasshoppers.

Portrait of fisherman after 6 fruitless hours of fly casting for Dolly Vardens.   Same nimrod after being kept waiting for breakfast for 3½ minutes.

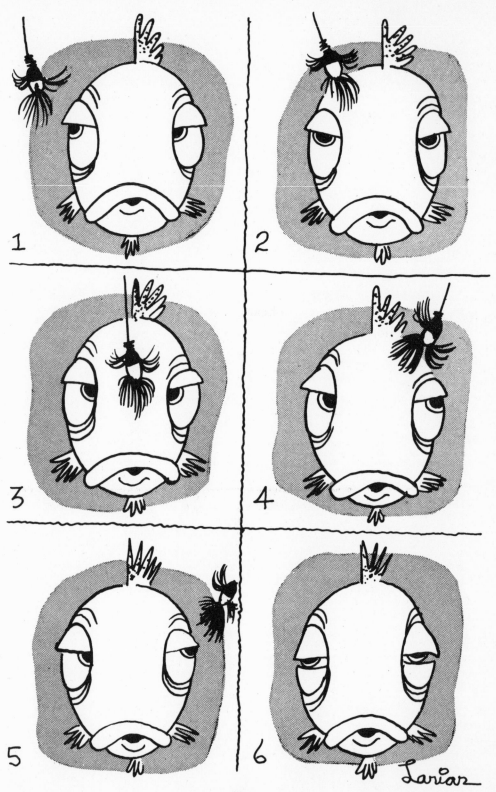

SURF FISHING CAN BE FUN (?)

They also serve who only stand and wait.
Henry Wadsworth Carp

There are thousands of simple folk who feel that surf fishing is the most thrilling sport of all. Simple? Maybe they're just plain damned fools, when you get right down to it. The average surf fisherman is cast in a special mold, but his name is legion.

When interviewed in the reception room outside the schizophrenic ward, a specially molded nimrod said: "My name is Legion — Ordway Q. Legion. I am a run of the mill type of man, aged thirty odd, with a good complexion, open pores, and plenty of you-know-what. In twenty-five words or less, I like surf fishing because. Like other devotees of the sport, I am also fond of waiting for street cars, theatre tickets and for my ship to come in. Anybody who can't learn to stand on his own two feet for more than five hours at a stretch is not worth his salt. Surf fishing requires lots of moxie, stamina and patience. Show me a seasoned surf fisherman and I'll show you my birthmarks. Yours very truly, Ordway Q. Legion."

This rejoinder is typical of all enthusiasts of the surf. When pinned down and pressed for an explanation of their favorite pastime they are inclined to balk, stutter and fumble for words. This comes about because no logical reason has yet been discovered for the sport. Surf fishermen are born and not made.

This same rule applies, of course, to Mongolian idiots.

Surf fishermen, unlike human beings, will cheerfully do without sleep and food, enduring freezing winds and broiling sun to pursue their favorite lunacy. On any day, along certain secluded stretches of sandy beach, a handful of these hardy souls can be found staring out at the waves and picking their noses. For hours on end, they cast their lines into the breakers and await the tug that means that something has grabbed their bait. The routine surf fisherman is quite happy if he gets one such jerk a day.

Two jerks will often cause him to emit light whinnies, and go off into spasms of high glee and abandon.

Three jerks can mean a bad heart attack.

HOW THE SURF FISHERMAN LOCATES HIS FISH

The beginner in this sport is quite likely to approach the water at any point. This comes about because all parts of the surf look alike to him. The expert, however, sees many things of interest before his sharp eyes. When cornered and browbeaten for this information, he will outline his strategy in this way:

1: *Look for the sea gulls!*

Anybody with half an eye can spot at least half a sea gull. The presence of these birds is supposed to indicate that there are fish below them. Nothing could be further from the truth. Male gulls soaring around are usually on the prowl for high-flying girl gulls.

Female gulls, by the same token, are probably only looking for buoys.

2: *Find some white water!*

If there are no gulls around, the surf fisherman next tries to locate some white water, or "white-caps." This usually indicates the presence of a sand bar, shoal, or the early stages of an onrushing hurricane. If no high winds develop, you can assume that you've found yourself a good sand bar.

Now look for a break in the bar. The best way to spot an opening is by wading out and probing with your fishing rod. For extra rough water, use extra rough fishing rods. For deep water, take swimming lessons.

If you've been lucky enough to find a break in the bar, you may be sure that the incoming water will carry lots of fish through to the landward side. Test this spot. Keep testing it.

If nothing happens after two or three seasons, maybe you'd better try another location.

3: *Locate a tidal current!*

Tidal currents produce eddies, rips, swirls, whirlpools, shallows and deeps. Shore fish are supposed to enjoy rips and will frequently be found at eddies, even when Eddie isn't home.

Specially designed portable surf casting seat for easily fatigued surf fishermen.

The biggest and smartest fish are often damned fools about going around in whirlpools, where they just drift around the bar like human beings, snatching tidbits along the way. If you are baited up with the proper snack, even the most drunken bass will snatch your offering while cruising around an offshore bar.

4: *Try roaming around!*

In the event that there are no gulls, white water, tidal currents or offshore bars, your last recourse is just strolling. Sometimes a casual stroll along the beach will earn you a little known fishing spot.

Other times, working your way along the shore may bring you from Long Island to the coast of Maine.

For details of what to do in Maine, consult the Maine Chamber of Commerce.

Have you absorbed all the hints and tips you just read about Surf Fishing? Think you're ready to make the grade? Before dashing madly to the nearest shore, ask yourself the following questions:

PROBLEM 1

You are fishing all alone on the beach. You cast your line and feel a terrific tug. But, after reeling in, you discover that you've hooked a young lass in a Bikini suit who resembles Lana Turner.

(*a*) Would you throw her back? _____

(*b*) Suppose she preferred to stay? _____

(*c*) Could you continue fishing? _____

(d) Even with the doll on your lap? _____

(e) Even if she began to kiss you? _____

(f) Are you kidding? _____

(g) Have you had your head examined lately? _____

PROBLEM 2

You are still alone on a beach. Suddenly a huge breaker washes up a 50 pound striper, slightly dead, but not yet decomposed.

(a) Would you throw her back? _____

(b) If you kept the fish, would you say you caught it? _____

(c) Who do you think would believe you? _____

(d) What on earth made you such a liar? _____

(e) Do you always call your wife such names? _____

"He's working for me!"

EXTRA!
OLDEST FISHING CARTOON ON EARTH
DISCOVERED IN ANCIENT TOMB!

My recent excavations in the Black Hole of Calcutta have at last borne fruit, gentlemen! After what seemed ages in the B H of C, I emerged at last with the famous slab of granite, recognized by many experts as the oldest cartoon extant. Hammacher, Soames and Finch insist that the art work is of the Babylonian, or post-Pubic, Era. On the other hand, Hart, Schaffner and Max claim it as a genuine etching of the Cretan stone mason named Heppelthwaite.

Heppelthwaite, however, insists they're all crazy.

"They are all crazy," says Heppelthwaite, in his now famous volume entitled: *Why Hammacher, Soames, Finch, Hart, Schaffner and Max Are Crazy.*

By completely ignoring the above-mentioned experts, I was able to discover the true facts about the famous stone. It was really the work of an ancient Egyptian cartoonist by the name of Kluck Gable, who created the drawing as a favor for King Rameses XI, an Egyptian potentate who loved to fish for eels on the lower Nile. The careful student of piscatorial life will immediately notice that practically no eels are represented in the work of art. But that comes about because there are practically no eels at all in the Nile.

King Rameses enjoyed the work of his cartoonist for a short time only and then Gable fell into sudden disfavor. Many Babylonian scholars think that the cartoonist was caught adding mustaches to dames in the royal harem. This is far from the truth, since records prove that Gable was discovered with his easel down while sketching one of the King's concubines. For this malfeasance, Gable was treated to seventy-seven lashes, after which the unfortunate artist was drawn and quartered into seven slices and buried in his own house.

To this day that little Egyptian cottage is known as the House of the Seven Gables.

Which brings us right back to Gable's work of art, whether you like it or not. Since the death of the now legendary cartoonist, his drawing of the four fish has made his name famous wherever cartoons are printed. His cartoon was published widely through the Roman Era, the Renaissance, the Post-Renaissance, the Age of Reason, the Age of Industry, and right up to the Age of Nuts, Bolts and Rivets. Conservative estimates tell us that down through the centuries the joke has been drawn by over 400,000 cartoonists, all of whom claim it as their own, original creation.

This is sheer nonsense. I think I have proved that the cartoon is one of the oldest wheezes ever printed.

That's why you'll never find it in *this* book.

ANGLEWORM: A smart-aleck nimrod who knows all the angles.

AN EASY GUIDE FOR CATCHING FISH

No fishing book would be complete without a large section devoted to developing the author's ego. Here the piscatorial writer usually lets his hair down and becomes a real "pal" to his reader, allowing him to peek into the author's personal "kit bag" of baits and lures, tricks and wiles. The result of this editorial freedom has led to a rash of strange formulae for hunting down fish. The fact that the fish mentioned exist in such places as Upper Nigeria, Outer Mongolia and Iceland does not seem to bother the ambitious writers of these dandy suggestions. A survey of the latest books on fishing reveals such charming essays as:

"With Creel and Cork to Catch the Gambodian Gunnysack."

"How I Snared my Saskatchewan Squid."

"Down Flatbush Avenue for Brooklyn Blowfish."

"Jigging for Juggernauts off the Jutland Jetties."

"Snagging Mussels with Doughball and Davit."

"Piranha Ahoy!" or "There Goes My Good Right Arm!"

Any reader who expects to find such frothy morsels between these covers had best run, not walk, back to the bookstore for a refund. This book concerns itself only with those finny friends well known to the man in the street. Here you will find an easy-to-follow, step-by-step guide to practically nothing at all. The odd facts and foibles recorded here represent a cautious peek into the customs and *mores* of a few of the well known specimens in local waters. This does not mean, however, that the fish can be depended upon to act according to my prognostications. After all, if fish were that reliable they would resemble humans and you'd be able to catch them every morning by offering them toast and coffee.

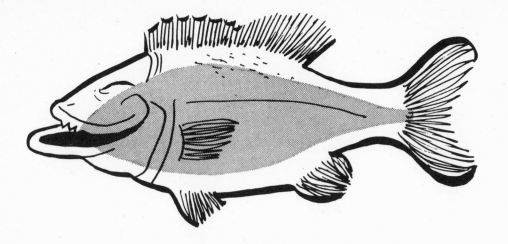

LARGEMOUTHED BASS *(Micropterus salmoides)*

Also known as Bigmouthed Bass, Loudmouth Bass, or Senatorial Bass.

Description

This greenish-bronze colored fish with the big fat lips is often mistaken for its cousin, the smallmouthed bass. They both hang out in the same pools and lakes, but this is only to confuse fishermen. The best way to tell them apart is by a close examination of their mouths. When found together, the largemouthed bass is always doing the talking. The smallmouthed bass, however, never hangs around to listen. He is much too busy feeding his face to bother with small talk.

Largemouthed bass, living in clear, light-bottomed water have clear, light bottoms. They also have an irregular horizontal black line running along their bodies from head to tail. Nobody knows why.

Characteristics

It is important for you to know the feeding habits of this fish, if you ever hope to catch one. Try to remember these simple facts:

A: In the morning the largemouthed bass comes into shallow water to forage for food. He gets up pretty early every day and likes to eat a hearty breakfast. Since he is pretty sleepy at this hour, toss your fly right under his nose and wait for him to spot it. If he sniffs it and moves off, don't lose your temper. Try to give him something he really enjoys on the next cast. Remember, he just stepped out of bed and is likely to be fussy.

B: As the sun heats up the lake, bass like to hide in cooler, deeper nooks. It is here that they do their mating, browsing around for a passing lady largemouth. To distract them from this pastime requires skill, patience and know-how. A passionate bass won't move away from his girl friend come hell or high water. You won't get anywhere at all with flies now. Try dropping a hunk of live bait his way, off a bobber. If this fails, you might bait cast with lures that go down deep. Make the lure very attractive. Put yourself in the bass' place at moments like this. An amorous bass would have to be half-wit to forget his sex life for some free lunch. Would you?

Tackle

A hungry bass will eat bass bugs, popping lures, bass flies, or even vagrant mosquitoes. For fishing deep, try for a bait that might lure the fish away from lovemaking. A live minnow hooked under the dorsal fin will sometimes work. If the minnow is sexy looking, that is.

Size

Bass caught in northern waters are not as large as southern bass. This comes about because of warmer water in southern pools. Southern bass just lie around all day and eat. Northern bass are much more active, like all other damn Yankees.

Diagram of Largemouthed Bass having a political discussion with a timid trout.

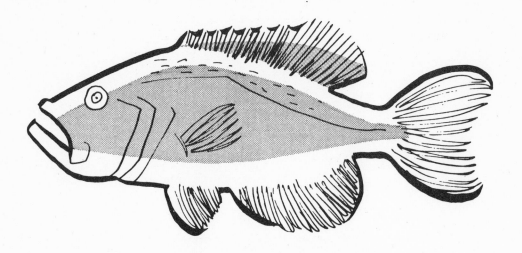

CALICO BASS *(Pomoxis nigro-maculatus)*

Also known as Black Crappie, Crappie, Green Bass and Papermouth. Some fishermen call this the Strawberry Bass. These people are either completely color blind, or awfully fond of strawberries.

Description

Anybody familiar with calico can usually identify the Calico Bass, which never seems to confuse textile men, dress manufacturers and apron salesmen. It has an olive-green body color and is black on top, with sides spotted liberally with black. The fact that its fins and tail are also spotted often confuses myopic anglers who complain of spots before their eyes when staring at the fish.

Characteristics

The Calico Bass isn't called "Papermouth" because it eats the *New York Herald Tribune*. (Nor is it called "Crappie" because it plays dice.) The fact is that the Calico Bass is a weak-chinned type of fish, with a soft mouth and absolutely no strength of character. This makes for difficulty, since the average Calico Bass would just as soon have you catch only his lower jaw which he will leave on your hook while taking the rest of his body to parts unknown.

Like most other pan fish, the Calico Bass swims in schools and prefers the company of others with receding chins and harelips.

41

Tackle

Use any light tackle, baited with live minnows, worms, grasshoppers, crickets or caterpillars. A #4 Carlisle hook is supposed to be perfect for the jaw of a Calico Bass. Be very careful when tugging your catch to the surface of the lake. Otherwise, Calico Bass will give you his lip.

Size

The average Calico weighs only about a half pound. After removing scales, fins, innards and head, this leaves only one small mouthful for frying. Hungry nimrods should seek out other bass.

The Calico Bass is still called "Crappie," — despite its negative reaction to dice.

SMELT *(Osmerus mordax)*

Also known as Candlefish and Icefish despite the fact that the normal Smelt has never burned a candle or had much truck with ice.

Description

Some fishermen think the Smelt got its name because of negligence in its personal hygiene. This is a ridiculous idea, since this fish smells no worse than any others.

Other theorists imagine that the name came about because of the Smelt's smeller. A careful consultation with many leading ichthyologists has convinced me, however, that the nose of this fish is just as useless as any other underwater sniffer. Smelt in an experimental tank, when confronted with garlic, onions or bad cheese, simply gulped the junk and showed no change of expression. A few of the leading ichthyologists reacted the same way.

Except for its coloring and its name, any junior Smelt can easily be confused with a trout. It has a slender, silver-sided body with a greenish tint, large scales and a forked tail. It gets along well with other fish and has a cool, steady disposition, good habits, and an even temper. For these, and other reasons, the Smelt isn't interested in changing its name.

Characteristics

Smelt are really salt-water fish which come into fresh water to spawn in the spring. They are a gregarious type of fish and like to run up feeder streams in mobs, the males and females rubbing shanks indiscriminately, but with great passion. Smelt can also be caught in the winter by fishing through the ice. So can colds.

Tackle

Smelt are often very fussy about what they bite. Try using a 6 foot level nylon leader and a #10 Sproat or Carlisle hook with light tackle. If this fails, rig your line for trout. This will flatter the Smelt, if he's the social climber type.

Size

These are very small fish, but are considered an epicurean delight by nimrods with small appetites. The average Smelt should be pan fried until it is a golden brown and then smothered in ketchup until it is a blood red. You'll need at least two dozen Smelt to feed a family of four. For a family of eight, multiply by two. For a family of sixteen, better try fishing for tuna.

Accurate snapshot of smelt's smeller (right) sniffing snout of suspicious salmon.

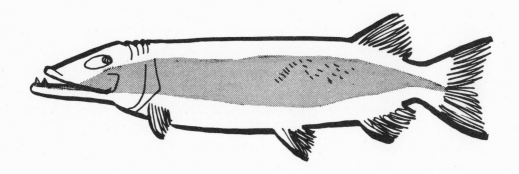

MUSKELLUNGE *(Esox Masquinongy)*

This fish has about fifty names, all of which are variations on the same theme. It has been called: Muskinonge, Lunge, Mascanongy, Noscononge, Maskenosha, Kinonge, Great Pike, and etc. ad infinitum and ad nausea.

Amateurs, who hope to land one of these some day, hopefully refer to the fish as a "Musky."

Seasoned fishing liars, too, pretend they've already landed one by calling it "That Big Musky Bastard!"

Northern Indians, who catch Muskellunge every day, are likely to call the fish "Ugh Phung," which means "The Great Stinker My Squaw Uses for Chowder."

Description

Despite the fact that the Musky is just an overgrown member of the pickerel family, it has no scales on the lower part of its cheeks. Nobody seems to know the reason for this phenomenon, which has been puzzling ichthyologists for generations. This doesn't seem to bother fishermen, however, since they've never really figured out the reason for ichthyologists.

The Musky's color varies, even among fish taken from the same lake. They don't appear to want to move around much, but will sometimes remain near a favorite bit of cover for a whole season. As they grow, they take on the same color as their surroundings. A Musky found up against grass may be pale green. The same Musky in deep water still looks bilious.

45

Characteristics

After mixing with Muskies for many years, I have come to the conclusion that they are much smarter than people. Without benefit of press agents, advertising men or advance publicity, these fish manage to paralyze every sportsman who comes their way. A clever Musky will pass up all kinds of bait, pretending to be fussy. He will turn down underwater plugs, natural suckers, and specially colored lures. But just drop over a cigarette butt on an ordinary hook and you're liable to have a real fight on your hands, mates.

The experts say that most Muskies grab only items that wriggle and squirm on the surface of the lake. The experts also say the lure should leave plenty of bubbles and foam in its wake. This is just plain silly. The average Musky is interested only in food and can be snared and subdued by way of a skillfully dropped salami sandwich.

Accurate diagram showing an average nimrod in the process of creating a 20 pound prevarication about the 2 pound Musky he has just caught.

Tackle

The sporty way to land these devils is with medium-weight bait casting equipment, using a rod with plenty of backbone for the task. Some of my best friends use fly-rods. But then, some of my best friends are rich. Only a man with a big bank account can afford to lose a half dozen fly-rods to catch one Musky. For the poorer, or "cheapskate" nimrod, a heavier rod is recommended. (For the really poor, see my essay on "Tickling Trout" — Page 112.)

After landing your "Old Evil Eye," make sure to have the correct equipment for subduing him in the boat. I always carry a baseball bat on my Musky expeditions. A well aimed crack between the eyes will usually quiet one of these beasts. Make sure to use a quick, downward motion when batting a Musky. A strong, upward motion will often slam the fish yards from the boat, thus earning you a two base hit, but depriving you of your catch.

Size

Nobody ever caught a small Musky, despite the fact that they exist as babies, children and teen-agers. The average Musky should weigh about fifteen pounds, but will increase in size and poundage as you lie about it.

THE BARRACUDA

I've never found a fish that's ruda
Than the oafish Barracuda.
Beware when round this wretch you linger
— He'll bite your bait, your toe or finger.
    Just between us, I would suna
    Pass him up — and fish for Tuna.

ATLANTIC SALMON *(Salmo salar)*

Also known as Kennebec Salmon, Parr, Smolt, Grilse, and just plain Kelt.

Description

Atlantic salmon are not pacific. They have short tempers and are colored blue and silver with red, orange and black spots on their sides. When angered, most salmon see the same colored spots before their eyes. Some salmon may have black "X" marks on skin. This "X" simply marks the spot. Nobody knows what for.

Characteristics

Like the Pacific salmon, the East Coast type also ascends fresh water streams to chase the girls. But unlike the Westerners, the Eastern type doesn't exhaust itself to the point of death in its first encounter with the opposite sex. Clever adults just horse around and take it easy. For this reason, they live to spawn several times.

Very old male salmon have been known to fight off young bucks for the privilege of hanging around the ladies. This does not bother the females, who are not fussy at all.

The Atlantic salmon is called by several names at various periods in its life span. A *parr* is a very young salmon who lives in a stream but won't make the trip to the sea. He has pinkish spots all over. This is just his way of blushing.

When the *parr* stops blushing, he heads for the sea and is then called a *smolt*. When addressed by this name he often starts blushing again, and you can't blame him. Once in a while, a *smolt* returns to fresh water

48

before manhood. He is called a *grilse* when that happens. Ichthyologists can not account for this habit of name-calling, which only occurs in the salmon family.

An adult salmon who has spawned is called a *kelt*.

An adult salmon who has not spawned is called a sissy.

Tackle

Salmon are easy-going fish who will bite at almost anything. A *parr*,

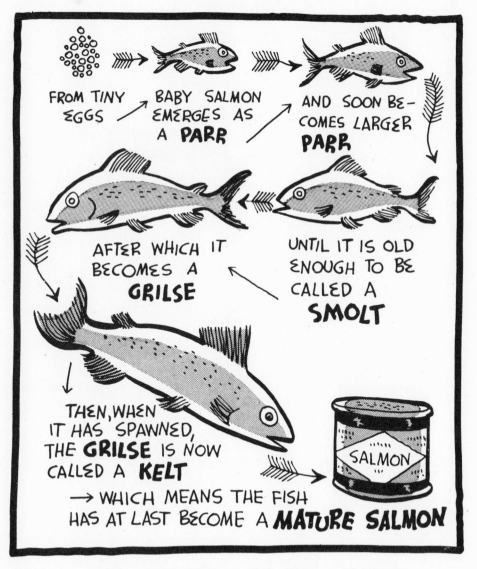

FROM TINY EGGS — BABY SALMON EMERGES AS A **PARR** — AND SOON BECOMES LARGER **PARR**

AFTER WHICH IT BECOMES A **GRILSE** — UNTIL IT IS OLD ENOUGH TO BE CALLED A **SMOLT**

THEN, WHEN IT HAS SPAWNED, THE **GRILSE** IS NOW CALLED A **KELT** → WHICH MEANS THE FISH HAS AT LAST BECOME A **MATURE SALMON**

SALMON

THE LIFE CYCLE OF THE SALMON

D

when hungry, will grab artificial flies. A *smolt* will nibble even the worst looking streamer flies. A *kelt* is pig enough to dine on clams, crabs, and even passing *parrs* and *smolts*.

The average Atlantic salmon weighs about 15 pounds.

You can see why. They eat too much.

THE SALMON

I hesitate to be unkind
But the salmon has a one-track mind.
Once every season, full of fire,
He swims upstream, higher and higher,
From dawn to dusk, and dusk to dawn,
From morn to night and night to morn,
> Up rocks and rills,
> Up streams and hills,
> Up high cascades,
> Up grassy glades,
> Up canyons steep,
> Through water deep,
> Up stones and rocks,
> Up dams and locks,
> From day to night,
> From dark to light,
Until at last, on one bright dawn,
He gets there — just in time to spawn.
> Now, having done his salmon duty,
> Now, having wooed his salmon cutie,
> And weary from the trip uptown,
> In quiet shallows he will drown,
> > Pondering, with his dying bubble,
> > Just why is sex so damn much trouble?

"There's a man to see you — on business, I think."

CHANNEL CATFISH *(Ictalurus lacustris)*

Also known as Channel Cat, Silver Cat, White Cat, Pussycat, Speckled Catfish, and Fiddler. They like to slop around in mud, and are sometimes called Dirty Slobs for this reason.

Description

The Channel Catfish, like the common house cat, has no scales. Right there the similarity ends. The whiskers on the Catfish's mouth are equipped with taste buds specially designed for underwater dining. It has a white belly, usually mud-stained from sleeping in the muck and mire. Its real color is olive-blue. When it cleans up for a date, this shade looks real pretty. At all other times, Catfish look like bums.

Characteristics

Most Catfish like to eat at night. They are not fussy eaters and will snatch at anything that happens to drift by them, including other Catfish. Their natural foods include such things as fresh-water clams, minnow, worms, crayfish and stuff like that. A normal Catfish will gulp his food and ask no questions. This habit leads to bad digestion, emotional upset and a surly disposition. It serves him right for having such bad table manners. You'll never catch a pickerel acting that way.

Tackle

Channel Catfish require a long-shanked hook of the O'Shaughnessy type. If O'Shaughnessy can't lend you his hook, try Hiram Chook, up on the next block.

Catfish anglers specialize in their own baits. Legend has it that Catfish will bite quickest when bait is foul-smelling. To make your own stinking bait attractive to catfish, you must use doughballs. These are created by simply mixing flour and water and boiling it in small pellets until finished product resembles buckshot.

Now place your doughballs in the garbage can for about ten days. This will give them savory, keen smell which all Catfish seem to enjoy. If you can handle your doughballs after ten days in a garbage can, they aren't quite ripe enough for Channel Catfish. Allow doughballs to remain in garbage can until neighbors complain of the stench.

At this point, doughballs are ready for fishing. But are you? To render yourself insensible to the smell, you must (a) stop breathing through your nose, (b) develop a bad head cold, (c) purchase a small Army surplus gas mask, or (d) go fishing for trout or bass.

Size

Channel Catfish run up to 25 pounds in weight. They make pretty fair eating. If you can forget about those doughballs, that is.

Normal Catfish reacting to fresh water clam.

Same Catfish reacting to succulent morsel of garbage.

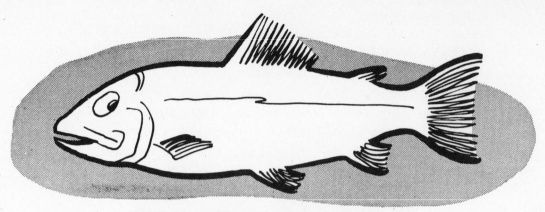

BROOK TROUT *(Salvelinus fantinalis)*

The Brook Trout is also called Squaretail, Brookie, Native Trout, Mountain Trout, Red Trout, Speckled Trout and Coaster. The fish, however, does not answer to any of these names.

Description

The exact color of the Brook Trout depends on the type of water from which the fish has been taken. Brook Trout in dark and muddy brooks have dark and muddy complexions.* Sometimes the Brook Trout changes color according to the food he eats. When fed on spaghetti and tomato sauce, the fish will break out in red and white spots. After dining for one year on this diet, most Brook Trout will get stomach trouble. Can you blame them?

---

*The same fish in clean water still won't wash his face!

Scientific study of common trout (with practically no brain at all) turning up its nose at a hand made fly created by a college professor (whose brain has been requested by the Smithsonian Institute after his demise).

Characteristics

Brook Trout prefer deep, cold water and can usually be found lurking under rocks, banks, fallen trees and stuff like that. The Brook Trout lurks because he is considered the shyest fresh-water fish known to man. He has a reputation to uphold.

That's why most fishermen are so quiet when around Brook Trout. A heavy footstep, a small cough or belch, or even a whistle in your nose can scare this fish out of a year's growth of scales.

Tackle

Begin by using fly-rod outfit, with level line and leader and nymphs, wet flies or streamers on #8 or #10 Sneck, Sproat or Carlisle hook. If this fails, try dry flies with tapered line and leader.

If this fails, try #9 barnyard angleworm on any ordinary sliced shank hook.

If angleworm fails, go home. You are in an area of very shy Brook Trout who will stop lurking only for other (female) Brook Trout.

Intimate close-up of average male and female Brook Trout engaging in a passionate love affair.

CARP *(Cyprinus carpio)*

Also known as German Carp. Especially in Germany.

Description

The carp is a big, ugly looking character, dirty and disreputable because he just doesn't give a damn. It has a small head and just enough brains to get along. It has a long, single dorsal fin. This would look perfectly lovely on other fish, but looks like hell on a carp. The adult of the species has two small "feelers" projecting from its upper lip which hang down and drag in the mud all the time. This doesn't improve the fish's appearance and is only admired by other carp of the same sloppy nature.

Characteristics

Carp breed as freely as rabbits, but don't hop around so much.

They flourish in streams, lakes, ponds and brooks and have been known to thrive even in old beer barrels. It makes no difference where a carp hangs out, so long as he can find a female around. Once a male carp locates his mate, he makes slow, sly passes at her. This does not frighten the lady carp, who is too damned lazy to swim away from him.

The inevitable result of her laziness is more carp.

Carp have been accused of many crimes, including cannibalism, mayhem and murder of the offspring of other fish. Actually, this is a big lie circulated by various sly and conniving fish who think carp are revolting enough to be convicted of anything in the book.

Tackle

Carp are wary. They are fussy eaters, despite their sluggish natures, and prefer worms or doughballs which they sniff and nuzzle before biting. Once hooked, an enraged carp will fight for his life and jerk your line around a bit.

Never underestimate a carp. They may be dirty slobs and ne'er-do-wells, but like all professional bums, they hate to be disturbed.

Size

The record for carp stands at 42 pounds, but they make good eating at any weight. Some people fatten carp by keeping them alive in a bathtub for a few weeks and feeding them lots of bread. This is all right for folks who don't like to bathe.

Bathing with a tub full of live carp can be a ticklish proposition.

Comparison chart proving that average ugly Carp isn't much worse-looking than average ugly nimrod.

MAN-EATING SHARK *(Carcharadon glaucus)*

Also called: White Shark, Killer Shark and Dirty Stinker.

Description

The shark is one of the biggest fish afloat today. It is also one of the hungriest. Estimates prove that the average shark consumes ten times its own weight in food every week. This does not include human beings who happen to be swimming by.

Some sharks come in light shades of blue and gray, delicately tinted and decorated. This has absolutely no connection with their dispositions, which are always nasty. Sharks have lots of teeth, but must turn over before biting anything above them. They don't seem to mind the turnover because of the overhead.

Characteristics

Most sharks find it hard to get along with mackerel, porgy, cod, haddock and other sharks. A hot-tempered shark will rarely pause to reason things out before biting anything. He just moves in and gnashes his teeth, gulping down enemies, friends and passing strangers without discrimination. This does not make him very popular with anybody. A real hard-boiled shark, however, doesn't give a damn. He lives a rather lonely life.

But he's always well fed.

Tackle

Never tackle a man-eating shark.

Close-up view of man eating shark.

THE FLOUNDER AND THE FLUKE

The flounder and the fluke are gruesome,
A flat and floppy, foolish twosome.
    The fluke will flounder when you net him,
    The flounder flips and dares you get him,
A floundering fluke will flail and flounder,
A floundering flounder's not much sounder,
    Unless by some fluke, a flounder feels
    You'll throw him back — and fish for eels.

FIDDLER CRAB: A wily old hardshell, often quite attractive to Ladyfish.

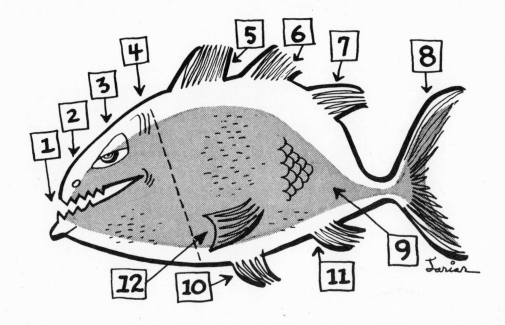

HOW TO TELL A FISH FROM PRACTICALLY ANYTHING

A recent poll of nimrods taken by the Nimrod Poll Corporation has proved to me that most fishermen are ill-equipped for pursuing the sport. If you think I'm kidding, try this simple test for yourself. Just waltz up to any fisherman, tap him lightly on the dorsal fin and ask the following question:

"Just exactly what *is* a fish, Bub?"

Your average angler will twitch and squirm and fall into a state of coma at this simple inquiry. He will turn all shades of red, stammer and stutter, cough, belch and make odd, bubbling sounds in his throat. He will throw up his hands, drop his rod, mop his brow and then fall into a cold sweat.

When pressed for a quick rejoinder, the more vocal nimrod will undoubtedly mutter:

"A fish? Well, now, let's see. A fish is a thing — um — sort of a long and funny looking item, kind of slimy and caught with a hook."

Obviously such sportsmen should be quickly packed in rock salt and shipped off to limbo post haste. The description could well fit my Uncle

Fulding, who happened to be a long and funny looking item of the slimy variety, and was indeed caught with a left hook by my Aunt Zenobia more times than can be mentioned here. The fact that most fishermen can't even describe the thing they are hunting for explains the fact that they rarely, if ever, catch it.

In response to the crying demand for a description of a fish, I've borrowed the accompanying diagram from the National Board of Piscatorial Pulchritude. It is essential that *all* anglers be able to differentiate between a fish and my Uncle Fulding. A few hours of patient study with this chart should prove a boon to all serious nimrods.

As Isaak Walton so aptly put it:

"He who knows not ye shape and ye sizes of ye wee fishes, does not merit ye name of nimrod."

(The italics are mine. So is the quotation. Isaak Walton rarely spoke to *anybody*.)

JUST EXACTLY WHAT A FISH IS

To start off, a fish consists of only two parts: the head and the trunk. Since a fish has no neck, it's pretty hard to tell where the head ends and the trunk begins. A line drawn from the fish's eyebrow (4) to the pelvic fin (10) doesn't help at all. To tell the head from the trunk, look for the part that has the teeth (1). If the fish has no teeth, look for the mouth. If the fish has no mouth, send it to the Smithsonian Institute at once. They've been looking for mouthless fish for years.

The shape of fish varies, but the most characteristic form is elliptical, or ovoid. This description fits almost every fish but the eel, which is long, slender and much too thin to be sexy looking. (Forget about sexy looking fish. It's much too early to be bringing up sex, anyhow.)

To measure the average fish, hold tape from mouth (1) to the end of the caudal fin (8). Fishes with long, protruding jaws are measured to include bad dentures and orthodontia. Make sure your specimen is inert before using the measuring stick. Fish, like human beings, don't like to be measured until ready for the grave.

1: Jaw, Mouth, or Mandible

Every fish has a jaw, mouth, or mandible, which he uses for eating, sucking, or just sneering at lures. Many have *vomerine* teeth, on the vomer bone in the roof of the mouth. Others have *pharyngeal* teeth, on the inner region of the gill bars. Sometimes it's hard to tell which type of dentures your specimen has. When this occurs, simply take the fish to your dentist.

2: Nostrils

Most fishermen are inclined to scoff at the idea of piscatorial nostrils. Nevertheless, most fish are equipped with the things, usually tiny holes through which they can detect the presence of bait, weeds and females. Most fish can smell pretty good. Especially after being left in the sun for a while.

3: Eyes

The eye of the fish is well developed and consists of the same general structure as the human optic. The fact that male fish can't wink doesn't seem to affect their love life. They can still ogle female fishes.

Most fish are badly nearsighted.

This doesn't mean they patronize opticians.

4: The Brain

Ichthyologists tell us that the fish's cranium is infinitesimal compared to the size of its body. A catfish weighing as much as a man has a brain about as large as a thimble. This isn't the only reason catfish can't sew.

5:6:7: The Dorsal Fins

These are spiny things stuck away up on the back. According to latest scientific findings, dorsal fins serve no purpose but to prick fishermen's fingers when landing their catch. Most fish have one or two of these things.

Reason for three of them in the diagram is that my pen slipped.

8: Caudal Fin, or Tail

This section of the fish is important for reasons of locomotion. To gain speed, the caudal fin is swished back and forth in the water. The average fish makes at least 57 swishes a minute while in low gear. For high speed, multiply by five and deduct the loss of headway due to vibration, bad steering and rocks in the way.

A fish usually keeps swishing his caudal fin even when standing still, relaxing, or courting his girl.

Nerves, probably.

9: The Scales

Fish have four types of scales: *placoid, ganoid, cycloid and otenoid.* No matter what you call them, they are always slippery as hell. You can easily determine the age of a fish by the number of scales on his back. Simply count them all carefully and then divide by the length of the caudal fin, making sure to include the caudal *peduncle.*

If you can't find the caudal *peduncle,* you have only yourself to blame. It's there, all right.

10: The Pectoral Fin

Just another fin.

11: Anal Fin

Still another fin, down under the soft underbelly. There's nothing at all interesting about this fin. Unless you're interested in the fact that ANAL spelled backwards is: LANA.

12: Ventral, or Pelvic Fin

The last fin you'll hear me mention.

Close-up of veteran nimrod telling the truth.   The same fisherman in the act of telling a monstrous lie.

("... No need to take an umbrella, dear — it'll never rain today ...")

"Aw, come on — I'll bet you swim like a fish!"

FISH CLEANING CAN BE CHARMING

There are two schools of thought on the subject of Cleaning Fish. The names of these schools are: (1) The North Brooklyn Institute of Piscatorial Surgery and Fillet Slicing, and (2) The South Cantonese College of Cod Cutting and Scaling. Since I am a graduate of both of these dandy seats of higher learning, I am willing to go out on a limb all the way for the Chinese School of fish cleaning.

My old professor, a shaggy seer named Subgum Q. Chowmain, must be blamed for my unpatriotic attitude on the subject. Old Subgum taught me to love his method of cleaning fish. The Chinese system is as follows:

A—Grasp fresh caught fish firmly by tail.
B—Get stewpot, frying-pan or broiler.
C—Place fish, scales and all, gently on pan.
D—Cook until done.

Any intelligent fisherman will see immediately that this method eliminates fish scalers, fillet knives, and loss of fingers. The orientals think that fish stewed in their own scales retain important juices and subtle flavors. Most American fishermen would be quick to agree with old Subgum, since cleaning fish can be the lousiest job of work known to man. Most American housewives, however, insist on lacerated fish for their frying pans. It is for this reason that I include the following simple four step cleaning procedure for all nimrods who happen to be married:

1. REMOVING THE FINS:

Begin this operation by carefully studying your fish. Most fish have small, wing-like appendages up around their heads, called fins. Grasp these gimmicks in your left hand. Now borrow your wife's sewing scissors. Cut off the fins. At this point, your wife will emit a loud shriek. She will demand that you buy her a new pair of scissors for sewing. She will complain that she can't finish her dress for fear she will smell like a fish market. Do not argue. Instead, add sewing scissors to your tackle kit and buy her another pair. (Average cost: $3.98).

2. REMOVING THE SCALES:

Most fish have lots of scales, all of which must be taken off before cooking. Operation requires use of Fish Scaler of inexpensive variety. Now grab fish and hold the beast down flat on bread board. If your wife

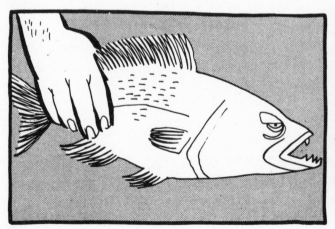

How right hand of average fisherman looks before
cleaning fish.

Same hand after
cleaning fish.

yells about using bread board, try kitchen sink. If wife yells about kitchen sink, remove any door in the house. Now sand down door to slick surface. Any reasonably good door can be converted into nice, large fish board. Best door to take is one between kitchen and living room. Removal of this door will give house a more modern, up-to-date appearance, but may require refurnishing kitchen and dining room. (Average cost: $764.24).

3: REMOVING THE ENTRAILS:

This is the easiest operation of all. Simply cut down edge of fish, on soft underside from neck to tail. Now close eyes and grope for entrails. Place entrails of fish in garbage can. Most beginners will drop a few entrails on kitchen mat, on way to garbage can. If wife objects, use damaged mat in your rowboat. Replace kitchen mat with fresh one your wife will enjoy. (Average cost: $4.34).

4: CUTTING OFF THE HEAD:

Now you are ready to use the sharpest knife in the kitchen. Clutch fish in right hand. Start long, straight incision from point slightly behind fish gill to spot right under fish neck. Be very careful when cutting

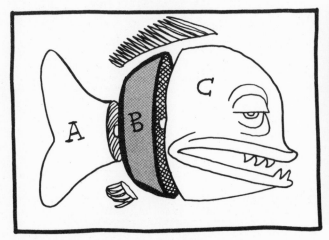

Correctly sliced fish, showing: (A) Tail, (C) Head, and (B) edible portion.

Diagram showing final size of edible portion.

through the backbone. Pretty terrible accidents can happen here. If this occurs, wash bleeding finger in soapy water at once. Have your wife tie tourniquet until the doctor arrives. Do not thrash about on way to hospital in ambulance. Insist on novocaine while stitches are being sewed in fingers. If doctor recommends short vacation, stay away from any resort featuring fishing. Rest and quiet will heal the wound. (Average cost: $134.50.) (Average cost, if you take wife along: $254.67.)

"Of course I cleaned the fish — I scrubbed them with soap and water!"

("Hand me that knife — any moron can clean a fish! . . .")

BUYING BAIT CAN BE EASY?

The Bureau of Fish and Wild Life has been in a perfect tizzy since I returned from my last survey of nimrods along the waters of Great Stinky Creek last Whitsuntide. Equipped with only a small pad, a pencil, and a boat named the *John Foster Dullest,* I ventured alone into the slipstream to hurl important questions at the assembled fishermen.

"What, in your opinion, is the most annoying problem facing the modern fisherman today?" I hurled at more than a gross of anglers.

The invariable rejoinder spat back at me was: "Bums like you with stupid questions! Beat it, Buster, you're scaring the barracuda!"

Packing these rejoinders in my handy creel, I journeyed to visit Dr. J. Edgar Hovering, my neighborhood psychiatrist, who was quick to come up with a handy analysis. According to the professor, nine out of ten eager fishermen suffer from a common ailment, namely: *Nili piscatorum,* a Latin colloquialism that means simply: No fish!

This leads me directly to the subject of bait, but don't ask me how I got here. Statistics reveal that the number of salesmen peddling bait now exceeds the fifteen million mark. This is a pretty disturbing figure when you backwater to realize that there are only fifteen million fishermen to buy the bait offered for sale. Simple arithmetic shows that this situation must cause a crisis among the bait salesmen, who find themselves sitting around and fingering their worms while thinking up ways and means for swindling vagrant customers. My breakdown of these bait bustards, recently submitted to the Federal Bureau of Bilvalves and Bustards, contains the following hints and tips for the alert angler:

THE "OLD TIMER" TYPE OF BAIT SELLER

This interesting character can usually be found loitering around piers, docks, wharves, waterways, bays, inlets and cul-de-sacs. The skillful nimrod can recognize the species from a distance of 342 feet, or sometimes less, depending on the direction of the wind.

The "Old Timer" type is usually over sixty, with shaggy ears and a nose hanging vertically down from between two sharp and piercing eyes. He can be spotted immediately by the costume he wears. You'll find him sporting an ancient mariner's hat, tilted jauntily over his left ear. Fifty per cent of these sea dogs are called: "Cap." Others like to be addressed as: "Skipper." The rest are either: "Pop," "Gramps" or just plain "Dad."

Typical group of "Old Timers" to be found in bait stores along the Eastern Seaboard.

The "Old Timer" salesman is an expert at getting rid of whatever surplus bait he happens to have in stock. An unsuspecting fisherman out for a day's flounder fishing will usually wind up angling for cod or haddock, depending upon the stock of bait in the "Old Timer's" bin. The sales pressure is applied with the skill of a Barrymore, as witness the following dialogue, caught on my tape recorder while hiding behind a barrel of clams in YE OLD TIMER'S BAIT BISTRO, on the shore of my local canal:

OLD TIMER: *(with gusto)* "Mornin', son! Great day for fishin', ain't she?"

CUSTOMER: "Sure is, Pop. Got any flounder bait?"

OLD TIMER: *(Laughing loud and long because he has no flounder bait left)* "Did you say flounder, son? Haw!"

CUSTOMER: *(Embarrassed)* "I hear they're catching hundreds of them up Guggle Creek."

OLD TIMER: *(Laughing louder)* "Ain't seen a flounder in Guggle Creek since the hurricane of '96, sonny. Any man tells you he caught a flounder lately, why that varmint's a downright liar."

CUSTOMER: "But it was Lester Smoldy. Lester's my best friend —"

OLD TIMER: *(Slyly)* "Maybe Lester told you that because he wanted all the weaks for himself, sonny."

Young Crud bait salesman disposing of $1.98 fly in less than five minutes.

CUSTOMER: *(Taking the hook)* "Weaks? Where?"

OLD TIMER: *(Leaning in conspiratorially)* "I hear they're catching ten pounders over in Noonan's Elbow."

CUSTOMER: *(Excited now)* "They are? That's for me, Pop. Got any weakfish bait left?"

OLD TIMER: *(Who happens to have 57 pounds of shrimp on hand.)* "Just so happens I got a couple o' pounds left. *(He wraps up five pounds of shrimp.)* You got yourself any weak hooks, son? Leaders? Stuff like that?"

CUSTOMER: "Left my tackle home. Thought I'd be fishing for floun-ders." *(Now the Old Timer proceeds to sell him one dozen Special Weakfish Hooks, one half dozen Special Nylon Weakfish Leaders, one dozen Special Weakfish Swivels, one Special Chumming Box for Weakfish bait, one Special Weakfish Chumpot, and a Special Weakfish Rod and Reel.)*

OLD TIMER: "That'll be exactly $46.78."

CUSTOMER: *(Paying the bill gladly)* "Thanks for the tip, Pop."

OLD TIMER: *(Blushing like a fox)* " 'Twarn't nothin', sonny."

(Curtain)

More expert Old Timer getting rid of $3.64 worth of decaying shrimp in less than three minutes.

As the curtain descends, we observe the eager and hopeful customer speeding madly to Noonan's Elbow, where he will anchor in the current and proceed to toss away $7.89 worth of weakfish bait to the crabs and blowfish.

THE "CHARMING CRUD" OR "SCIENTIFIC" BAIT SELLER

The Charming Crud is usually a blood relative of the Old Timer who owns the bait shoppe. He may range in age from 17 to 42 and is equipped with a saucy smile, sincere optics, and hot and cold statistics on any detail of fishery. In one quick flip of his bright magenta eyes, he will assess and appraise his customer down to the last quid in the fisherman's buskin. He is quick on the trigger and a fast man with the adjectives and adverbs, as witness the following playlet, caught on my portable dictaphone:

THE CRUD: *(Respectfully)* "Good morning, sir. It looks like an excellent day for piscatorial pleasure. The presence of cirro-stratus over the horizon presages a clear, cool and sparkling day on the water."

CUSTOMER: *(Impressed)* "It does?"

THE CRUD: *(Warming to his task)* "Indeed it does, sir. I might add that you'll do well with bass today. Bass are eager to bite when the cirro-stratus appears in the sky."

CUSTOMER: "That's good news. Have you got an inexpensive Gold Ribbed Hare's Ear, size ten?"

THE CRUD: *(Mildly astonished)* "Are you serious, sir?"

CUSTOMER: "I'm in dead earnest."

THE CRUD: *(Laying a Hare's Ear on the counter with a sigh)* "You're the boss. But this is the first Hare's Ear I've sold in the past five years, believe it or not."

CUSTOMER: *(Suddenly doubtful about the Hare's Ear)* "What's wrong with Hare's Ears?"

THE CRUD: *(With sincerity)* "They just don't work in this neck of the woods, sir. A recent survey by the State Board of Fisheries shows that our local bass got sick and tired of this kind of fly. Ichthyologists claim that the bass have tired of all Hare's Ears because the region has been invaded by the Horn-tailed Chump, an insect that all bass seem to favor. The influx of the Horn-tailed Chump has led us to design a special fly to resemble it."

CUSTOMER: *(Fascinated)* "Have you got any in stock?"

THE CRUD: *(Now he lays a gaily festooned fly on the counter. This monstrosity resembles a purple gnat, a green nymph, a yellow caddis and a common horse fly, all rolled into one.)* "Here you are, sir. We call this the Arrogant Parmezan Stableboy Moron."

CUSTOMER: *(Impressed)* "Hmmmmmmm. Sure is a pretty name."

THE CRUD: *(Warming to his chore, now)* "The Arrogant Parmezan Stableboy Moron is more than just pretty, sir. It's guaranteed to catch any fresh-water fish alive today. And if you switch to salt water, it will catch flounder, fluke, tuna, cod, haddock, bluefish, porgy and Bess."

CUSTOMER: *(Eagerly)* "I'll try a half dozen of them."

THE CRUD: "That will be exactly $7.99."

CUSTOMER: *(Paying out willingly)* "Thanks for the tip. You've been a great help."

THE CRUD: *(Blushing like a young fox)* "Nothing at all, sir. I assure you, it was nothing at all."

(Curtain)

As the curtain falls we see the fly fisherman running to the nearest stream where he casts the Arrogant Parmezan Stableboy Moron into the water approximately five thousand times and catches (a) one itinerant sunfish, (b) one small rusted beer can, and (c) a bad cramp in both legs.

COOKING AND STEWING IN
THE GREAT OUTDOORS

It was Mark Twain, the great American humorist, who said: "Everybody talks a lot about fish. But nobody ever really does anything about them."

This is not as funny as it sounds. Or is it? The fact remains that ever since man discovered the delight of jerking fish out of water, he has been faced with the serious problem of getting rid of his daily catch. Current estimates show that millions of fish are caught daily and Sunday, during the height of the season. Which leads us directly to the core of our problem. What is to be done with the millions of fish caught this year? A breakdown of the horrendous statistic, when put into cold print by the accounting firm of Breakdown, Horrendous and Statistic, looks something like this:

Approximate total number of fish presented to relatives, friends and neighbors after a day on the water 102,367

Approximate number of fish refused by relatives, friends and neighbors 102,367

Number of fish thrown into garbage pails 354,980

Number of fish palmed off on local cats 563,786

Number of fish stuffed by taxidermists to be hung on den walls because of great size 1

Number of fish thrown back for personal reasons 675

Total number of fish cooked, fried, broiled and eaten (not by cats) 56

The basic reason for such a tremendous loss of food lies in the personality of the average fisherman. He will spend a small fortune on tackle and bait. He will rush madly to the fishing grounds and torture himself by overexposure, sunburn, windburn and heartburn. And for what? To keep 563,786 cats loaded to the seams with fish.

If more men knew how to cook, such a situation could easily be remedied. No longer would the weary nimrod spend extra hours in an attempt to palm off his catch on unappreciative friends, neighbors and relatives. By learning a few simple rules of outdoor cookery, you, too, can whip up a quick fish dinner.

As a public service, I've gathered the following basic outdoor cooking recipes for the use of all amateur chefs. (In case of cramps, remember to run, do not walk, to your nearest antacid dispenser.)

HOW TO FRY

Indoors or out, the easiest way to cook fish is by frying. This process requires a very hot flame, which may be hard to create in the woods. To manufacture a really torrid fire, I usually carry a small can of kerosene along on all fishing trips. If kindling wood does not flare up and get hot, pour on about a pint of kerosene. Make sure to step back quickly after pouring. Stepping back slowly may broil your fingers. This is a waste of time, since broiled fingers are not edible.

Once the flame is burning brightly, drop in a good supply of vegetable oil, grease, butter, or bacon fat. When the fat begins to smoke and smell up the locality, this is a sign that the pan is ready for your fish.

Now drop your first slice of fish into the fat. If the immediate area becomes sprayed with the flying grease it is a certain sign that your fat is really hot enough. (Grease stains on clothing can be removed with carbon tetrachloride.)

((Grease stains on flesh are not stains at all, but blisters.))

(((To ease the pain of blisters, always carry a first-aid kit.)))

A standard method of gauging the heat of your frying pan is by watching that first slice of fish carefully. An overheated pan of hot fat will completely brown the fish to a crisp, asbestos-like delicacy. A generous covering of ketchup should help make the morsel palatable.

Always save your used fat. It comes in quite handy when cooled, for treating those burns and blisters on the way home.

STEAMED FISH

Here is an ancient recipe for creating a delicious fish dish:

First, clean the fish carefully, taking care to remove all guts. Steamed entrails are not very tasty.

Now season the corpse with salt and pepper.

Wrap the fish in greased paper, then in an old newspaper. Any daily type will do, even a tabloid. If you can't find a newspaper stand in the woods, locate a corn field and use corn husks, thoroughly saturated in water.

Next lay this little bundle in a bed of ashes and stir up the fire. Fifteen minutes later, yank out the corn husks. If you can find them. If the fire has not completely burned the husks, you should discover a delicious, tasty, steamed fish cadaver.

Never mind what it *looks* like. Eat it. The small coals surrounding the fish are only burned slices of wood, or ashes. This will supply your body with much needed carbon. Outdoor cooks who do not happen to need carbon must find other fish to fry.

PLANKED FISH

This is an old favorite of Indian guides and needs only a hardwood board, or a slab of timber that has been smoothed on one side. To make such a slab, begin by cutting down a good sized tree. Now hack the trunk into thick sections, using a cross-cut saw for the operation. Sand down the lump of wood carefully, making sure to eliminate loose splinters. These splinters can be used later as toothpicks, but will stick in your throat if eaten with the fish.

Split the fish in half, leaving the belly skin unbroken. Then tack the fish to the plank, using small carpet tacks and tack hammer for the operation.

Now stand the whole thing up alongside a bright, roaring fire. If the plank begins to burn, you have chosen the wrong tree for the board. Start again, searching for Oak, Cherry, or Hard Maple.

When exposed fish begins to turn flaky and white, it should be lifted away from flame and eaten.

Remember always that the plank may still be hot when you lift it.

Fishermen with burned hands from lifting hot planks can still enjoy planked fish, if fed the delicacy by other fishermen in party without burned hands.

BROILED TROUT

All this needs is a small, portable broiler rack. The best type can be borrowed from your wife's kitchen stove for the day. If your wife sees you taking her broiler, try the local hardware store.

Clean and split the trout down the middle, making sure to grease the broiler wires so that hot fish won't stick. It is advisable to do this operation when broiler is cool. (For finger burns and other ramifications, see: Planked Fish, above.)

After scraping broiled trout off broiler wires, add a soupçon of squeezed lemon to the remaining shredded debris.

Lemon will improve the taste of any fish.

Even this one.

BOILED POTATOES

Potatoes in this simple form are always the staple diet of all woodsmen cooks. Anybody can boil a potato, and usually does. All you need is a small pot of water in which to drop your "spuds." Use potatoes of uniform size. Do not ever remove jackets of uniforms, which contain all the vitamins, starches, buttons, pockets and eyes. Make sure that potato skins are scrubbed thoroughly, using good sized scrubbing brush with strong backward and forward motion. Remember that too much scrubbing will injure the skin of the sturdiest potato, causing welts, abrasions and ugly lacerations.

Always boil up a few extra potatoes for tomorrow's meals. When served cold, old potatoes may be flavored with practically anything.

No matter how you do this, the result is always called potato salad.

But don't say I didn't warn you.

FAMOUS FISHING FABLE (START)

No fishing book can ever be complete without including the age old yarn about the experienced fisherman and the stupid fool.

Here we see the seasoned angler doubled up with laughter at the silly amateur who thinks he can catch a Musky with a drop line, a sinker, and an old flounder hook.

"If you catch anything with that rig," exclaims the veteran, "I'll pay you a buck a pound!"

After which, the shy beginner only gulps and walks away.

FAMOUS FISHING FABLE (END)

Here we see the arrogant angler about to shell out exactly $45.00 to pay off for the 45 pounds of Musky the inspid amateur has landed.

"How in hell did you do it?" wails the veteran. "I fished all day with special plugs, lures, spoons and flies. I tried every bait in the book. What did you use?"

"Nothing at all," admits the fool. "I just hit them with the oar and dragged them in. For a buck a pound, I didn't have time to experiment!"

HOW TO BE HAPPY THOUGH
FISHING IN SALT WATER

Every once in a while during the dog days, a frustrated fisherman friend will burst into my office, his face a mask of woe, his eyes red with sorrow, his unrestrained tears splashing into my inkwell.

"No fish," he blubbers. "Ten hours in the bay and no fish. What am I going to tell the little woman?"

After a brief rubdown by my Senegambian houseboy, and a square meal from my oblong food freezer, I give the damned fool the address of the nearest fish market and send him reeling off into the night.

It is incidents like this that started me thinking about the many problems of the salt-water fisherman. If the whole tribe of them were laid end to end, they would form a straight line twice around the globe, marching two abreast over the Ural Mountains and winding up with enough left over to fill the Yankee Stadium during the World Series, despite the fact that most anglers would rather fish than watch baseball.

Wherever our coastline kisses the sea, you will find thousands of these sportsmen dropping their lines, baiting their hooks, nibbling stale sandwiches and slurping lousy coffee. Many of them have never fished in fresh water. But loads of them have never bathed in it, either.

They flock to the sea because it teems with piscatorial life. And some-body told them that you don't have to pay for a license. This results in an attitude of sweaty anticipation among beginners, who imagine that they will return home staggering under a load of flounder, porgy, fluke or bass. For this reason, on any week-end fair or foul, our local inlets, bays, docks, piers and harbors are jampacked with a gang of energetic lunatics who dash willy-nilly from one bad fishing spot to another, hoping against hope that they will be lucky enough to bring home proof of their prowess. For this reason, too, many fish markets remain open quite late on Saturdays and Sundays and holidays.

It's about time somebody cleared the air for these unfortunate fisher-men, who seek the solace of fishing and peace and quiet in the outdoors, but wind up mumbling in their beards and racing to the nearest psychia-trist for counsel. Fishing in salt water can be quite easy, if you follow these simple directions:

BOTTOM FISHING

Bottom fishing means exactly what it says — fishing while resting on your bottom.

In order to achieve this comfort, walk, do not run, to the nearest sign that says: BOATS FOR HIRE. You will usually find an evil smelling shack nearby that houses an ugly looking character known as the "pro-prietor." For a few dollars down (a fifty dollar deposit and a second mort-gage on your house), this jovial juggernaut will allow you to use one of his leaky dories.

Approach the rowboat cautiously. Test it carefully, allowing your-self a half hour of quiet meditation while tied to the dock. If the boat doesn't sink during that interval, you are now ready to pilot it out into the channel.

Bottom fishing is a lark, provided you can locate a spot where the fish are lurking. Let's consider for a moment just what makes a good fishing ground. First, put yourself in the fish's place. (No, no, Elmer, there's no need to jump overboard!) Fish must eat in order to live and most of them will migrate to the nearest area that is rich in free marine lunch. A favorite snack bar for bottom fish exists around piers, rocks, jetties and bridges. But the best place of all is around a wreck.

CHUMMING

Here's a dandy way to attract the fish to the top of the water, should you tire of the bottom. To fish successfully by this method, you must first build your own chum box, like the one in the diagram adjoining. All you need is an old beer crate, a few feet of ½" wire mesh, and a few days off from work to construct it. Simply attach wire mesh to bottom of the box and create aperture on top. Now drop in shrimp, mossbunker, killies, beer cans, or anything else you want to keep fresh and cool. Some fishermen open a can of oily sardines and throw it into the chumpot. This often attracts fish fond of nibbling on tin. Other fishermen suggest dribbling dry oatmeal in the water to lure fish who haven't had breakfast.

Still others recommend boiled rice for any Chinese fish who may happen to be in the vicinity.

Diagram showing how chum box can be packed to hold: (1) a dozen cans of beer, (2) 6 pints of rye, and (3) milk for hangover.

DRIFTING

This system is useable in bays, inlets and creeks where the tide runs strong enough to jerk you around. As the current slaps the boat this way and that, you should drop your baited hook to the bottom with a heavy sinker. This will occasionally bump into a lazy fish who is sitting around waiting for food to come his way. Impact of the sinker against the fish's

Interesting diagrams showing the correct fishing rigs for top and bottom fishing
— with the usual location of the fish in both cases.

cranium will either knock him cold, stir him into opening his mouth, or send him scurrying off into the mud.

Impact of a strong rip tide against your boat is quite likely to carry you out to sea. If this happens, simply add more line, freshen your bait and go deep sea fishing until the Coast Guard arrives to rescue you.

TROLLING

This is surface fishing, pretty much the same as drifting, except for the fact that it requires rowing, if the boat has no engine. To locate fish on the surface, watch the sea gulls. Intellectual gulls usually dip and swoop over schools of surface fish. Drop your lures into this area and troll slowly back and forth. Patience will reward you with either a good catch of game fish, or at least one gull.

JIGGING

Never jig in a rowboat. Not unless you can swim well.

Correct position of hook in killy, for
Fluke fishing.

Incorrect position of hook.

NATURAL NYMPH: Cute bug that has shed its outer coat.

WITH ROD AND HOOK THROUGH STREAM AND BROOK

The technique of fishing in streams and brooks may look easy to beginners. Amateurs, however, soon discover that most brooks must be analyzed and studied before dropping your line into a nest of submerged beer cans. Each stream seems to have its own personality and should be appreciated in the way that you approach a skittish female — slyly and with an end in view.

The accompanying diagram is a sample chart of a section of Old Muscletawny, a typical brook in the trout region of Upper Badsmell, New York. Can you chart the hazards? For the benefit of all myopic anglers, here's the lowdown:

1: OCCASIONAL ROCKS.

This type of formation is to be found in almost every stream in the land. Trout are supposed to favor dark holes under rocks like this. Intelligent anglers will cast *behind* the current, so that they can attract the trout on the way into the dark holes. Expert fly casters can put the fly just short of the rocks. Inexpert casters manage to land in the rocks time after time. This leads to loss of time, loss of hooks and loss of tempers. Stubborn amateurs who persist in losing flies this way are said to have: "Rocks in the head."

2: OCCASIONAL CATS.

Notice that angler is unaware of marauding bait stealer approaching the minnows in can. To avoid cats, bring along your dogs.

3: OCCASIONAL GAME WARDENS.

These characters are to be found on most streams and brooks. To avoid penalties — buy a fishing license. If you can't afford one, become a game warden yourself.

4: OCCASIONAL DEBRIS.

Diagram shows a submerged section of a 1927 Maxwell Sedan, with headlight in fairly good condition. This type of junk should be avoided, unless you happen to be fishing for a 1927 Maxwell Sedan headlight.

5: OCCASIONAL STUMPS.

Old trees are often lying around in the way of your hook. Sometimes the trout will play around the roots of swamps like this, nibbling at decayed roots. Don't try for these vegetarian fish unless you've brought vegetarian lures along in your tackle box.

6: OCCASIONAL FARMERS.

These lurking lice can be very annoying. Especially if you happen to be fishing on their property.

7: OCCASIONAL BATHING GIRLS.

Hazards like this are often encountered on streams close to summer resorts, etc. They can be hooked and landed if you have the equipment, but require special bait and a different type of line.

THE SARDINE, ANCHOVY AND SPRAT

To sardine, anchovy and sprat,
I raise my glass and doff my hat,
They sob not, neither do they grin
When washed down gullets bathed in gin.
Thus, sardine, sprat and anchovy
Fulfill a common destiny,
      They breed like rabbits, thank the Lord,
      And don't cost much as smorgasbord.

"Sure you put the bait on right, Emma?"

A FISHERMAN'S GUIDE TO FISHERMEN

TYPE NUMBER ONE: THE SOURPUSS

No fishing party is ever complete without at least one of this breed. He can be immediately recognized by the expression on his face: a mixture of gloom, boredom, dissatisfaction and just plain nastiness. Nobody knows whether this was caused by a birth injury, a sour stomach, or the fact that he married the wrong woman. The Sourpuss knows, however. He goes fishing regularly to escape her.

It's fairly easy to spot a character of the Sourpuss type. He makes his presence known immediately by resenting any decision the group makes. He will claim to be an expert at selecting bait, locating good fishing spots, fly casting, trolling, cleaning fish or chasing women.

Psychiatrists maintain that there is only one way to prevent a Sourpuss from ruining your fishing party.

Don't invite him along.

TYPE NUMBER TWO: THE SCIENTIST

The Scientist fisherman approaches the sport with the same study and concentration used by Professor Einstein in formulating his Theory of Relativity. (The fact that Einstein may go fishing with a diaper pin and breadballs makes no difference to the angler.)

The true Scientist fisherman believes that every detail of fishing must be considered before dropping his hook into the drink. He will begin by checking cloud formations, barometric pressures, tides, water temperatures and the psychic life of the fish he expects to catch. He will manufacture special lures and flies after a careful study of samplings of piscatorial stomachic debris.

Once under way, the Scientist will invariably migrate to a special geographic locale in which his calculations assure him that his quarry lurks.

After which he will cast his bait and catch no fish at all like the rest of us damned fools.

TYPE NUMBER THREE: THE HERMIT

This peculiar specimen engages in fishing only because it affords him an easy method for getting away from people. He can be found in stream, bay or lake, paddling his own canoe in the direction of nowhere in particular. He will drop his anchor in an isolated spot, drop his line, and then drop off to sleep. The fact that he can accomplish the same results by finding a cave, or climbing a tree, never seems to occur to him.

Some psychiatrists claim that the Hermit is closely akin to the Sourpuss in many ways. This is not true. The Sourpuss may hate people, but he likes to catch fish. The Hermit, on the other hand, just wants to be alone. He will often throw back his catch, especially after landing a noisy fish.

Exhaustive studies of the Hermit type prove that he is usually a man of middle age with a wife and seven kids.

This explains why he wants to be alone.

TYPE NUMBER FOUR: THE NATURE BOY

This rare breed of fishermen never quite got over the fact that it won a Merit Badge in Nature Lore while a member of The Green Panther Troop of the local Boy Scouts. Because of this background of knowledge of things piscatorial, he will tell you that he's really not interested in catching fish at all. Just *looking* at them, *fondling* them, or *sniffing* them is enough, he maintains.

The true Nature Boy insists that he goes fishing so that he can be closer to nature. He may drop his line and go through the motions of the sport, but he does this as a matter of form and doesn't really want to catch anything at all. Instead, he will finger the minnows and let the worms crawl gaily in his lap. He will make passing remarks to the seagulls and admire a passing flight of green flies.

At day's end, Nature Boy can be found in high spirits, a condition brought about by long hours of admiring the fauna and flora. The fact that he hasn't caught a thing doesn't bother him at all. "At least we were out in the sun and air," he will remark.

Other fishermen in the party (who have caught nothing, too) would do well to imitate his attitude.

G

TYPE NUMBER FIVE: THE CHAMP

Fishing expeditions that include this type of nimrod must be prepared for the inevitable complications brought about by the presence of the Champ. He is usually the athletic sort, having excelled in either football, basketball or quoits while in college. For these reasons he will immediately set about organizing various competitions for the group. These contests will include:

1: A prize for the first fish caught.
2: A reward for the heaviest fish caught.
3: A contest for the most fish caught.
4: A tournament for the first fish landed with blue eyes.
5: A race to catch the sexiest looking fish.
6: A battle to net the fish most resembling Chiang Kai-Shek.

After arranging these various competitions, the Champ then proceeds to win out in each struggle. His rewards are calculated to return him a substantial profit on the day's activities, a fact that rarely endears him to his companions.

Fishermen who do not like to gamble should avoid the Champ.

Fishermen who like to gamble should bring along their own bookies.

TYPE NUMBER SIX: THE OPTIMIST

The Optimist (or Laughing Boy) suffers from the painful illusion that he is a very comical character. His sense of humor, however, becomes an affliction to all the other members of the party since he has either already told his jokes several times before, or his audience has heard the same gags on the last Milton Berle television show.

The Optimist usually gathers a goodly number of fishing stories before each trip. From time to time, as the day progresses, he will dip into his storehouse of humor in this fashion:

When asked whether he's getting any bites, he will reply: "Bites? Hell, no — I'm just sitting here drowning worms."

When asked whether he likes codfish balls, he will say: "I don't know. I never attended any."

Hilarious comedy of this type can only be avoided by the following three methods:

1: Bring along a pair of earmuffs.
2: Get drunk on beer. After two quarts, any joke sounds good.
3: Stay home and listen to Milton Berle.

SPARE THE ROD AND SPOIL THE CANE!

A concise, easy to follow, step by step, peachy way for constructing your own Calcutta Cane Rod.

Attention, boys! Are you sick and tired of your old rod? Do you find it out of balance, rusty and corroded at the ferrules? Are you shocked and mortified by the cost of a new one? Do you wince, blush and feel shy and uncomfortable when unwrapping your rod before other fishermen? Are you irritable, touchy and short-tempered when asked sly questions about your equipment?

No fisherman need suffer any longer because of a bad pole. Among the most recent hobbies to spring up during the monsoon season last year was the sport of Rod Making, or Calcutta Cane Cutting. Nimrods have been getting pretty sick and tired of being rolled and mugged by equipment salesmen in tackle stores. A recent survey shows that there are more than 12,987 different rods now on sale. They begin at a fancy price and then go onward and upward until you need second mortgage money to buy one. Yet, even the best of them does nothing more than lower your line into the drink.

Any fool can make his own Calcutta Rod. To prove this statement, I have assembled my easy-to-put-together directions for your approval. Anybody capable of reading English can wind up with a new, fresh, beautiful fishing stick. Fishermen who want these instructions in French, Spanish, German or Ute will have to go elsewhere for their tuition.

STARTING YOUR CALCUTTA ROD

The first thing you'll need is a large slice of Calcutta Cane, either from your neighborhood Calcutta Cane Shoppe, or by fast freight from the Calcutta Cane Combine, in Calcutta, Wisconsin.

When your cane arrives you will find yourself gawking at a long thin stick, or pole, resembling nothing on earth but a long thin stick, or pole. Stand it up against the nearest wall and stare at it for a little while. This is important, because you must determine whether you've bought a male or female Calcutta stick.

The male pole is invariably stronger, sturdier, lustier and much more muscular.

The female Calcutta Cane is more pliable, easier on the eyes and much sexier looking.

It is important to select a stick free of all defects such as worm holes, cracks, pimples, wens and wrinkles. There is nothing more embarrassing when pulling in a "big one" than to find your fishing companions snickering behind your back and making sly innuendoes about "those dreadful blemishes" on your rod.

To avoid such comment, seek out all surface flaws before starting your rod. Eliminate all blackheads, warts, crow's feet and hangnails. The female Calcutta Rod is usually free of all such imperfections. The male is just a dirty slob and doesn't give a damn. After your rod is clean as a whistle you will be ready to cut it down to your personal size. Great care should be exercised here, since faulty tailoring of your stick can result in discomfort while fishing. You want a rod that feels good in your hands, not too long, not too short, but exactly right. If you are the small, squat and pudgy type with broad and heavy shoulders, thick wrists and thighs, you must cut away a good slice of the tip. If you are long, lean and angular with skinny arms, bony shanks and a pale, bloodless, sallow complexion, maybe you'd better see a doctor right now.

FINAL DIRECTIONS

1: Every fishing rod needs guides. These are the little metal holes through which the line will pass. Use a good ferrule cement to attach them to pole. Heat each one carefully. If too hot to hold in your hands, drop it. Fix burned fingers with butter or grease.

2: Wrap your guides around with a strong nylon thread. To secure the guides permanently to the stick, get some varnish and spread it over each winding. If varnish spills on rug, send rug to cleaners quickly.. Right now, before your wife gets home.

3: You are now ready to test your Calcutta Cane Rod. Bend it to a severe angle, applying about fifty (50) pounds of pressure on the skinny end. If rod bends but does not break, you are ready to fish with it. If rod cracks and breaks, maybe you'd better buy a cheap metal one at the tackle store.

QUESTIONS AND ANSWERS ABOUT CALCUTTA RODS

QUESTION: How can I make a good rod if Calcutta Cane is unavailable?

ANSWER: Good fishing rods can be made from the branches of good young spruce trees. If no spruce trees are available, try the Australian Ginger Tree. If no trees at all exist in your neck of the woods, try an old broomstick (without broom), or a small flagpole (without flag).

QUESTION: I followed your directions very carefully. When I was all finished, my Calcutta Rod looked like an old horse whip. Some of my fishing friends tell me you are a fake and don't know what you're talking about.

ANSWER: Your question shows you obviously cannot follow simple instructions. It is gross, vulgar and uncouth people like you who give the sport of fishing a "bad name." My advice to you would be to take up quoits, you moron!

QUESTION: Oh, yeah?

ANSWER: Yeah!

A FEW COMMON MISTAKES IN CALCUTTA
ROD MAKING

1: Open screen door has allowed mosquitoes in room. To avoid mosquitoes, spray body liberally with insect repellent. If you can't stand
insect repellent, work in a closet.

2: Radio is playing. This sort of distraction makes job tougher, especially if the band is playing a tango. You can't tango and build a
Calcutta Rod at the same time.

3: Tube of ferrule cement is leaking. This will prove a disadvantage
when the time comes to tie and bind ferrules.

4: Man is wearing heavy wool sweat shirt. Proper costume for the job
demands that worker operate in shorts and undershirt. Some men
work altogether in the nude. These people are called nudists.

NOTES ON BUYING A TACKLE BOX

Most fishermen would prefer to buy their own tackle boxes. This is practically impossible, however, especially if the fisherman happens to be married. Ninety-nine out of every hundred wives will buy their husbands a tackle box (a) for Christmas, (b) as a birthday present, (c) on Father's Day, or (d) just for spite.

One wife in each hundred will not buy her husband anything at all of this type. This is because she is a widow.

A good tackle box is made of wood or metal. Some experts say that wooden boxes can be built to withstand all kinds of weather and resist warping. These experts are damned liars. The only way to prevent warpage in a wooden tackle box is to take up carpentry. Then you can use the box to store nails and screws in. (If you do your woodwork in the cellar, make sure cellar is dry.)

Metal boxes seem to be the rage these days. They come in a variety of colors and are very pretty to look at. This condition ends after the first fishing trip. Rustproof boxes withstand the rust, all right. They also withstand corrosion, mildew and dry rot. What happens is, they just fall apart at the seams. To prevent this, you can: (a) paint the entire box with a mixture of waterproof, rustproof, corrosion proof paint, (b) remove all existing bolts and substitute heavy rivets, (c) remove all heavy rivets and substitute heavier rivets, (d) return tackle box to store for a refund, (e) buy yourself a few cases of beer with refund money.

Then, (f) stay home and drink the beer.

Tackle boxes usually come in four sizes: small, medium, large and just plain cumbersome. The larger the box the better, since it must contain the following essentials for every fishing trip:

1 pair smoked glasses	1 thermos bottle (qt. size)
1 can smoked glasses cleaner	5 comic books
1 pipe	1 pair reading glasses
1 pipe cleaner	6 sandwiches
1 carton cigarettes	12 paper cups
6 cans beer	1 box paper napkins
1 beer can opener	1 jar pickles (medium)

This leaves practically no room for a few fish hooks, flies, lures, sinkers, etc. For these items, the experienced fisherman will equip himself with a fishing jacket containing the customary eight to fifteen pockets.

Or why not try a paper bag?

THE SMELT, THE WAHOO AND THE CRAPPIE

The smelt, the wahoo and the crappie,
Have little reason to be happy,
But still, despite their appellations,
They all have dandy reputations;
The smelt is svelte, the crappie, snappy,
The old wahoo is game and scrappy.
Yet crappie, smelt and wahoo, too,
Would just as soon be called: *"Hey, you!"*

WHAT THE WELL-DRESSED FISHING
CATALOGUE WILL WEAR

The fishing world was rocked back on its heels after my recent return from a journey of exploration through the great sporting equipment store of Aberwormy, Twitch and Fallow.

Unbeknownst to none but a few thousand intimate friends, I entered the giant emporium through a side door on the afternoon of June 16th, 1953. From there on in, it was bedlam, mates. Once alone in the jungle, I made the trek single-handed, through every inch of veldt and swamp, deep into the inner recesses and aisles, beset at every turn by native salesmen who lunged at me with all manner of barbed verbiage and blandishments.

Once, in a steaming section of Boots and Shoes, your correspondent found himself almost trapped and sold down the river into the white slave market at Rangoon. But patient plodding and a keen nose for the smell of exit doors brought me back to civilization at last. Four days and three nights later, burning with a high fever, I groped my way out into the darkened streets of New York. I had done the impossible. Aberwormy, Twitch and Farrow hadn't sold me a single item of sports equipment!

I pass on my findings for what they are worth, anglers. If Aberwormy, Twitch and Fallow had their way, all fishermen would dress in the manner illustrated in the accompanying diagram. The composite picture was created out of the mass of scientific data culled from the garnering of over five (5) pounds of catalogue material I grabbed on the way out of the store. It's all yours, at bargain prices:

1: DRY FLY FEDORA:

This natty number comes equipped to hold 5 Black Gnats, 12 Blue Duns, 35 Gold Ribbed Hare's Ears, 23 Parmachene Belles, 78 Wickham's Fancies, 45 Brown Spiders, 56 Hendricksons, and 765 Royal Coachman Fanwings. An important adjunct for all fly fishermen, these felts come in sizes from 4 to 9, with special crowns for all Mongolian Idiot nimrods. Available colors: Brownish green, Puce, Old Lavender and just plain Dung.

Priced for clearance $45.22

2: SPECIAL WEATHER FORECASTER:

Latest mechanical rain-detector invented to detect sudden squalls, blizzards and typhoons. Comes complete with radar unit contained in utility carrying case. Automatic alarm siren blasts warning when low pressure area passes zone of hat brim. Works on either AC or DC current.

Special throw away price $87.97

3: DANDY UTILITY KNAPSACK:

This handy closet is manufactured to hold up to 78 pounds of extra equipment, lunch, spare socks, boots, pup tent and baby carriage.

Fisherman Ernest Herringway says. *"I wouldn't think of going fishing without my Dandy Utility Knapsack. The last time out I was able to include one whole case of Scotch, a complete six volume set of guide books, and my wife Zelda."*

Knockdown price $1.98

4: GIZZLETON GAFF:

Manufactured by the famous House of Gizzleton, manufacturers of Giggs, Gussets and Gaffs, by special appointment to his Majesty, King Oog of Upper Nigeria. The Gizzleton Gaff is well known for its three-way prong, which makes it useful for spearing fish, picking apples and probing for lost coins through sidewalk gratings. A "must" for all red blooded fishermen

Sale price today $6.87

5: NEW WAY LANDING NET:

An important piece of equipment for the "modern" nimrod. Old fashioned landing nets can now be thrown away in favor of this model. Comes equipped with handy four pound hammer for beating fish over head when landed. Extra fifteen pound hammer for Hammerhead Sharks, optional.

A real bargain at $87.54

6: PEEK-A-BOO POCKET JACKET:

For the fisherman who loves pockets. This model contains over 50 specially designed places created to hold: Pipes, Tobacco, Pipe Cleaners, Toothpicks, Shaving Cream, Tooth Brush, Lighter, Lighter Fluid, Matches, Salt and Petter Shaker, Sandwiches, Rigs, Lures, Flies, Spoons, Knives Tablecloths, Pocketbooks, Spinners, Photographs, Newspaper Clippings, Caterpillars, Frogs, Grasshoppers, Nymphs, Glasses (sun and reading), and stuff like that.

For quick clearance $35.67
Same jacket with extra money pocket . . $45.67

7: COLD STORAGE CREEL:

Here's a peachy item for all anglers who like to take home absolutely fresh fish. Simply drop your catch into this handy ten gallon storage tank and forget about them. Fish will remain alive and kicking until you get home. Comes equipped with utility shoulder straps, liniment and gauze bandage for bruised pectoral muscles.

Our special price $65.89
With six fish $69.50

8: DEEP DIP WATER THERMOMETER:

Essential equipment for all fishermen who believe temperature of water controls habits of fish. Devised to register all kinds of reactions. Ice in brook will ring bell to warn nimrod of approaching frost. Steam valve will blast if Gulf Stream heats up. In normal temperature, entire mechanism dissolves in water, leaving fisherman free to fish unworried.

Priced low for you $15.23

9: ANTI-NOISE MEERSCHAUM:

Specially devised to eliminate sucking noise in most pipes, for fishing in area of shy and retiring trout. Guaranteed not to make a sound. Stem is stuffed all the way to mouthpiece with cotton batting. Bowl of pipe is completely jammed with asbestos filings, sand and gravel. Impossible to make a sound while smoking the Anti-Noise Meerschaum. Impossible to smoke, too.

Attractively priced at $9.98

10: COLLAPSIBLE BOOK REST:

For the literary fisherman only. Complete knock-down book stand can hold volumes up to seven pounds, at eye level. A delightful companion for restless nimrods who like to improve their waiting hours. A boon to all anglers who happen to be book reviewers.

Our sale price $1.34
With one volume of "Fishing Made Easy"   . $3.89

SURF CASTING: Trying to land one in the breakers.

YOU, TOO, CAN GUDDLE A FISH!

Any of you boys sick and tired of fishing the hard way?

Fed up with buying fancy rigs, bugs, lures and flies?

Do you feel run down when hit by a car?

See sprats before your eyes?

Then come with me, mates, but leave your rod and reel at home behind the umbrella stand, because all you need is the five fingers on your right hand. Or six, if you happen to be a freak. Few nimrods realize that our primitive ancestors first caught fish barehanded. The ancient cave man became quite adept at tickling trout and went onward and upward with the art after that until he was soon tickling catfish, black bass and young women.

You, too, can startle your friends by guddling a trout. They may laugh like hell when you squat down near your favorite brook to finger a fish. But their laughter will turn to sheer paralysis when you hand-grab a fifteen pound "big fellow" right under their very noses.

All you need do is study my simplified methods, gathered for your education after endless hours spent on my belly to discover the best ways to tickle fish plumb silly:

APPROACHING THE TROUT

After you've discovered your quarry, walk right up to him brazenly.* Make lots of noise. This will scare the fish under a rock. Now wade in and approach the rock very carefully. Make sure to take off shoes and pants before wading, please. Squeaky shoes will scare the trout badly.

Now kneel down and reach in your right hand very slowly until you feel the fish back there. Using the index finger cautiously, start rubbing the trout with an easy, provocative motion. A male trout of the bachelor type will appreciate your tickling him. A female trout will think her husband just got home. She will sigh and roll over gently into your palm. When you hear this sigh it means she's all yours. Now lift her out of the water and toss her ashore. She will die laughing.

Of course, it's absolutely necessary to seek out experienced, married type lady trout for your first guddling.

Virginal trout act sort of silly when tickled.

---

* It is suggested that all fishermen anxious to guddle fish should learn a few things about their quarry first. Once I went guddling for black bass. I found one under a large rock that grabbed my finger and damned near bit it off. The reason for this escaped me until I woke up in a nearby hospital.

Then the nurse told me I was suffering from a water moccasin bite.

Water moccasins do not approve of guddling.

Not unless they're guddled by other water moccasins.

THE COD

The lowly Cod seems doomed by fate
To decorate a dinner plate,
No matter what the path he takes,
He'll end his life as Codfish Cakes!

H

ARE FISHERMEN REALLY PEOPLE?

Many psychologists maintain that fishermen are among the most normal citizens alive today. This comes about because they have learned to endure all kinds of torment manfully, including sunburn, windburn, chilblains and indigestion while waiting for a nibble. Fishing is credited with developing patience, calm dispositions and a sense of humor.

Can you qualify as a good fisherman? The following test has been designed to measure your depth of character:

(Score 10 points for each "Yes" answer.)

1: Your wife wants you to go visiting relatives. You want to go fishing. Do you win out? (   )

2: After you've visited the relatives, do you still want to go fishing? (   )

3: Do you get mad when you can't catch anything but crabs? (   )

4: When you bring home the crabs, do you pretend you went fishing for them, instead of flounders? (   )

5: You are in a boatload of fishermen. Everybody in the group catches lots of fish. You catch only seaweed. Do you feel like throwing the other nimrods overboard? (   )

6: Ever feel like throwing *yourself* overboard? (   )

7: Can you swim? (   )

Group picture of: (A) Famous scientist, (B) Plumber, (C) Banker, and (D) Garbage Collector — all of whom tell exactly the same type of fishing lies.

8: Your friend Charlie Klunk is always bumming your cigarettes. Do you resent this? (   )

9: If not, how does it happen you're now smoking a pipe? (   )

10: Did you ever tell your wife a lie? (   )

11: When she found out, did you apologize? (   )

12: Are you still on speaking terms? (   )

13: How do you get along talking to yourself? (   )

SCORING YOURSELF

130 — If you've answered all these questions truthfully, you shouldn't have made such a high score. This proves that you are a fisherman by nature. Continued lying of this sort will not be resented by other nimrods who are just as untruthful as you are.

90 — This kind of score shows that you have a strong conscience, a deficiency that might make you honest if you don't watch out. The fact that you tell the truth only once in a while means you'd probably do pretty well at golf, too.

50 — A rotten score like this shows that you are ill-equipped for fishing. You lack confidence and seem much too weak mentally for the outdoors. Stay indoors and take up parcheesi.

20 — You are much too honest to be credible. This is often just as bad as being an expert liar. Most fishermen expect their pals to be expert liars. Practice on your wife, at least three times a week. Practice makes perfect.

HOW TO GO FISHING THOUGH MARRIED

It is becoming increasingly clear to all lovers of fishing that the sport will soon fade from the face of the earth unless drastic measures are taken. Statistics show that the average married man can only go fishing a few times a year. This comes about because of the average wife, who would much rather keep her husband at home mowing the lawn, changing sink washers or beating rugs.

Accordingly, out of my personal passion for the sport, I've devised the following tactics for harassed husbands who yearn for the rapture of piscatorial pleasures:

1: THE VOLUNTEER FIREMAN METHOD

This is a fairly simple way to get out of the house if you happen to live in a small town. The first essential is to contact your local volunteer fireman brigade and enroll at once as a member. Whenever the fishing bug bites, have a friend in the firehouse sound the alarm. When the alarm rings, grab fire fighting equipment in one hand. Grab fishing tackle in other hand, on way out of garage. (If the alarm rings at night, go night fishing.)

2: THE LITERARY METHOD

This is an excellent system for fishermen with a literary bent. Notify your wife that you are about to write a book about marine life. She will be proud of you at once. Tell her you must make occasional field trips to do research. Now you are free to go fishing whenever you like.

At the end of the season, tell her that your book was rejected by every publisher in the field. Nine out of ten wives will swallow this yarn. The tenth may call you a liar.

If married to the tenth, there's only one way out of the mess. Better write the book.

3: THE FRESH AIR METHOD

This is an easy method for all husbands who happen to be anaemic. Begin by complaining about your state of health. Develop a pasty, sallow complexion. To do this, stop eating, drinking and sleeping. After a few weeks of this, the little woman should notice your bony condition.

A visit to the family doctor will gain the required results. A good doctor will advise fishing as an aid for your general health. A friendly wife will follow his advice.

For perfect results, make sure your wife is friendly.

4: THE INFALLIBLE METHOD

Get a divorce.

BACKLASH: What often happens when you try the wrong line.

MY WIFE'S SPECIAL GUIDE FOR THE
USE OF FISHING TACKLE

FISHING ROD: This is an excellent item for beating rugs, carpets and small children who are naughty. Also successfully used for removing cobwebs from hard-to-reach spots on ceilings.

NYLON LINE: Very handy when you're out of string for wrapping gift packages. Comes in assorted colors.

FISHING KNIFE: A sharp-bladed instrument that can be used for cutting flowers, hedges and other foliage.

SINKERS: Small pellets of lead that come in various weights and make good ballast for weighing down bottom seams in curtains and draperies.

CREEL: When hung in pantry this is a handy container for potatoes, onions and other vegetables. Can also be used as a wall decoration with flowers and fern. Makes a nice mailbox, too.

FISH SCALER: Great for combing hair of all long-haired-dogs in need of grooming. For larger dogs, get larger fish scalers.

THE FISHERMAN'S HANDY
DICTIONARY

ALEWIFE: An alcoholic lady fish of the herring family.

ANGLEWORM: An *oligochaetus* worm of the *gena lumbricus*. This is just a fancy Latin way to describe one of those squirmy things found in damp earth behind the barn. Angleworms are usually sneered at by fresh-water fly fishermen, despite the fact that all fresh-water fish think they're simply *yummy!*

BACKLASH: A painful lashing on a fisherman's back, caused by casting bait inexpertly.

BAIT: Assorted stuff to put on hooks, usually purchased in Bait Stores and clearly marked as such despite stringent regulations by Better Business Bureau to control fraud, connivery and larceny.

BIVISIBLE: A two-toned fly with no wings but plenty of hackles. Bivisibles are popular because the angler can see where they float. The fact that fish never see them is unimportant.

BLACKFISH: A very dark fish.

BLOOD KNOT: A dandy knot that's supposed to hold your tippets together to form a tapered leader. Fishermen without tippets should try other knots.

BLOWFISH: A fish that blows.

BLUEFISH: A fish that is colored blue and doesn't blow.

BLOODWORM: A bait worm that bleeds easily. Bloodworms should be kept in damp seaweed to preserve their lives. Excellent bait for all fish that relish the taste of blood. Vegetarian fish won't touch them. Neither will vegetarian fishermen.

BOBBER: A floating hunk of cork, wood, balsa, porcupine quill or hollow plastic. Bobber jiggles when fish grabs bait and jerks. When this happens, fisherman quickly tugs on line. When this happens, fish abandons bait and goes home.

BOLO CASTING: The practice of casting a heavily weighted line from a pier full of fishermen. This often results in (a) getting your line way out beyond the others, (b) hitting a neighboring nimrod on the head, and (c) having aforesaid neighboring nimrod knock your block off.

BONEFISH: A very bony fish.

BONITO: A fatter fish of a different type, slightly bony in the name only.

CADDIS FLY: A *Trichoptera* having four wings and aquatic larvae. The caddis fly larva carries his house with him. This saves him the expense of buying a plot when he builds. Caddis nymphs usually live in the muck of streams. You can't honestly blame them.

CALCUTTA ROD: A long pole used for fishing by residents of Calcutta.

CALICO BASS: A fish that likes to eat calico.

CARP: A fish that doesn't care for calico at all.

CASTING: A method of getting hook and bait out far enough into the stream where fish may more easily avoid it.

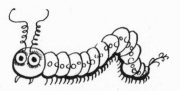

CATERPILLAR: Wormlike larva used as a bait. Usually found on twigs, flowers, grass, branches, and on the back of a fisherman's neck.

CHUMMING: The practice of fishing with one's friends in a drifting boat. (Also called *"bumming"* and *"slumming"* by fishermen's wives.)

CHUM POT: The pot of one's chum. A bay window.

CINCINNATI BASS HOOK: Type of hook used for catching bass in the vicinity of Cincinnati.

CLAMS: A bivalve mollusk variously called Quahog, Hardshell, Cherrystone, Soft-shell, Surf, Razor or Skimmer. Clams live in mud and won't come out unless urged. They make excellent bait for practically any fish because of their fine flavor. They are also good fried, steamed, or just gulped down. To make a clam stew, get a lot of clams and cook them as soup. To make a clam fritter takes too much time. Clams just don't like to fritter.

CLINCH KNOT: A peachy knot for attaching leaders to hooks, snaps and swivels. If this one's too tough, see: "Blood Knot." If Blood Knot is too tough, use Scotch Tape.

COD: A soft finned gadoid fish usually found in codfish cakes.

CRABS: A decapoda crustacean with a short, flattened carapace, a small abdomen and a bad disposition. Almost all crabs make good bait. The *green crab* can be caught while swimming, or you can attract them with old fish heads. Most crabs love to eat garbage, small fish and human hands and toes. The *Fiddler crab* lives in a hole and won't come out for hell or high water. He has only one large claw, but can bite twice as hard with it. The *Soft-shell crab* is as hardboiled as any of them.

CRAPPIE: A cute fish with a very nasty name, the poor thing.

CRAYFISH: Also called Crawfish. This is plain nonsense, since the fool thing is a crustacean and not a fish at all. Crawfish can usually be found hidden under rocks, have shiny eyes and no sense at all. Crawfish

can swim backwards with remarkable speed. This gets them nowhere, since they have already just been where they are going. You see what I mean?

CREEL: A willow or rattan basket used for transporting dead fish from stream to home. Can also be used as efficient mailbox when not fishing.

CRICKET: Small and noisy insect usually found under rocks. Trout will snap at these, even if only to quiet them.

CUTTHROAT TROUT: A yellowish trout with a murderous disposition.

DOLLY VARDEN TROUT: A pretty lady trout of the Varden family.

DOUGHBALL: A small wad of dough used as bait for catching the wily carp. To prevent the doughball from disintegrating on your hook, mix a little cotton with it. Wily carp will choke to death on cotton. Serves him right for liking doughballs in the first place.

DRAGON FLY: A large, ungainly insect preferred by fish with large, ungainly mouths.

DRY FLY: A phony fly made by fishermen who think trout will rise to the surface to nibble at it. A good dry fly must float on the water. A dry fly that sinks is called a wet fly. A few popular dry flies are called: Adams, Badger Bivisible, Blue Dun, Light Cahill, Gray Wullf, Hendrickson, Royal Coachman and Wickham's Fancy. These names are optional. The best dry fly I ever saw was called: Soupy King Flotsam Garbage-drag. It worked fine. I named it myself.

EEL: A very slippery fish that will sometimes travel halfway around the world to date his girl friend. Nobody knows what makes the eel so anxious. The fact is, he never returns to explain. And female eels never gossip.

FEATHER JIG: A crazy looking hunk of artificial bait that sometimes attracts crazy tuna and bluefish.

FLOATING PLUG: Another weird artificial bait, manufactured in 189,786 shapes and sizes for 189,786 customers who will take an oath they caught 189,-786 fish with the fool things, thus adding 189,786 fresh lies to the sport of fishing.

FLOUNDER: A flat fish that loves to lie in the sand and mud. From where he sits, he can look straight up at the bait, since he has two eyes on the right side of his head. This peculiar development makes him similar to a human. Thus, he is very sincere and also slightly stupid. The normal flounder will believe anything offered him is a tasty morsel. The normal fisherman isn't much different.

FLUKE: The same fish, with eyes on the left side of his head, a bigger mouth and a full set of dentures.

FLY: Any of a million manufactured insects designed to attract, tease and confound the stupid fish. Statistics show that damn fool fish have refused to bite no less than $5,234,879.54 worth of flies during a normal fishing season.

FROG: The best three frogs for fishing are called *Rana Clamitans*, *Rana Palustris*, and *Rana Pipiens*. These Latin frogs are guaranteed to catch any Latin fish in your brook. To catch American fish, use Yankee frogs.

GAFF: A long pole with a hook on the end, used for coaxing stubborn fish into boat. Also excellent for rescuing lost rods, reels, hats, coats and would-be suicides.

GOLDEN TROUT: A cute type of trout, first caught by a man named Percival J. Golden.

GRASSHOPPER: A high jumping insect said to be relished by certain fresh-water fish with gourmet tastes. Grasshoppers can usually be found in fields and thickets. To catch them in great quantities, grasshopper hunter should secure sexy looking Katydid. Katydid on small string will lure all passing male grasshoppers into your net. This is because of unsavory reputation of female Katydid. Male grasshopper remembers last encounter with attractive Katy. All he had to do was ask her. And Katydid.

GRAYLING: A stupid fish that's smart enough to convince fishermen he's a trout.

HADDOCK: The *Melanogrammus aeglefinus,* also known as "Finnan Haddie" on a Blue Plate Dinner.

HAIR BUG: An artificial bug made by simply tying hair around a hook. Bald headed fishermen can make this bug from old tou-

pes, mattress stuffings and collected barber shop sweepings.

HELLGRAMMITE: The immature offspring of the Dobson fly who live beneath stones and rocks in shallow streams. Hellgrammites have sharp mandibles, with which they love to bite passing protozoans, amoebae, and fishermen's fingers. Some hellgrammites can bite harder than trout. On fingers, that is.

HERRING: A learned North Atlantic fish that never moves out of its school. They can be found among sardines, shad and alewives, but look their best when pickled or with sour cream and onions.

HIP BOOTS: Very long rubberized or plastic boots, designed for fishermen who like to get themselves in deep water. Not to be confused with WADERS, which can take a man into water up to his armpits, after which he can forget about trout and go swimming.

HOOK: Once called the simplest equipment in the fisherman's tackle box. Originally designed and conceived to hold bait for fish to bite. Recent developments, however, demand that average fisherman know the following models: Sproat, Kirby, O'Shaughnessy, Virginia, Carlisle, Cincinnati-Bass, Chestertown and Sneck. Any of the above types can be hollow pointed, beak pointed, superior pointed or Dublin pointed. Small boys with limited mentality still use diaper pins for hooks. The fish don't seem to see any difference.

ICE FISHING: A silly business. Only fools fish for ice.

ICE FLY: An artificial fly used for fishing in sub-zero weather. It has large, soft hackles that move as the fly is jigged up and down. Jigging the fly is absolutely meaningless to the fish. But the fishermen keep warm if they jig.

JUNE BUG SPINNER: A June bug that spins.

JAM KNOT: A fisherman's knot with jam on it from Junior's sandwich.

JERSEY SPINNER: A resident of Pennsylvania who spins.

KILLY: A small bait fish sometimes erroneously called a minnow. Killies are very much like minnows and can be caught in minnow traps. Minnows can be caught in killy traps, too. When found together even their best friends can't tell them apart.

KINGFISH: A fish that's fit for a king.

LADYFISH: A female fish that has preserved her virginity.

LAFAYETTE: Also known as a Spot, a Goody, a Masooka or an Old Wife. Called Lafayette only at formal dinner affairs when served with French wine.

LEADER: In a fishing party, the man who always knows the "special spot" where the "big fellows" are hiding.

LURE: Highly colored thingamajigs painted the brightest tints and hues. Vivid reds, blues and yellows seem the most popular with anglers. Scientific studies prove that all fish are color blind. This makes no difference to fishermen, who buy them anyway.

MAY FLY: Small insects that may fly.

MINNOW: (See Killy)

MUSKELLUNGE: A very large Northern fish, called a "Musky" by fishermen who want to give the impression they've landed one. Also called Noscononge, Maskenosha, Kinonge, and Great Pike by other nimrods who aren't such liars.

MUSSELS: Small black shellfish found in good Italian soup.

NIGHT CRAWLER: A foolish character who leaves home before dawn to go fishing. Also a worm. Especially if he wakes his wife on the way out.

NYMPH: An insect in the crawling stage, usually found hiding in the muck or under stones, for reasons of its own.

O'SHAUGHNESSY: A good friend of the author.

PAN FISH: A term of disrepute, usually used by fishermen when discussing sunfish, crappies, rock bass and perch. Pan fish will take any bait, even small chunks of kneaded bread. They are caught mostly by young boys and girls, on drop lines, diaper pins, or bare handed. Sometimes experienced fishermen will use fancy equipment to fish for pan fish. At such times, they are caught mostly by young boys and girls on drop lines, diaper pins or bare handed.

PARR: A fish found on or around golf course ponds and streams.

PICKEREL: A small member of the Pike family that spawns only once, in the spring. After that, the Pickerel just sits around and makes faces at passing nimrods.

PORK RIND: An excellent bait for

sandwiches, if fish aren't biting.

PROPELLER SPINNER: An imitation propeller set on front and rear of certain lures to attract all fish with aviation minded attitude.

RAINBOW TROUT: A very pretty trout that is sometimes caught during rainbows. It can also be caught during hurricanes. But this doesn't mean you can call it a hurricane trout.

REEL: A type of spool used for winding up fishing line quickly and efficiently. Reels come in a variety of types, including: Arbor, automatic, bait casting, level wind, multiplying gear, salt water, single action, spinning and star drag, all of which manage to get loused up by backlash. To eliminate backlash permanently, fish with drop line.

REEL SEAT: A small chair on which extra reels are seated while waiting to be used.

SAND SPIKE: A surf rod holder for sleepy surf fishermen.

SANDWORM: A worm found in wet sand, mud, or under damp rocks. Sandworms have strong jaws and love to bite people

when being put on hooks. Once on the hook, however, they behave themselves and just bleed a little. They have a strong family resemblance to bloodworms, but not quite as much blood. Lack of vitamins, probably.

SAND STORM: A bad windstorm on the Sahara desert. (Included for Sahara Desert fishermen only.)

SHRIMP: A small, cute crustacean usually found in Shrimp Salad.

SINKER: A hard, inedible doughnut put into your lunch box by mistake.

SKITTERING: Fishing with a long bamboo pole and a string. Extensively used by frugal Scotch nimrods to eliminate cost of reels, lines, and wasted motion involved in other types of fishing.

SMELT: A small, highly edible fish that should have its name changed.

SMOLT: A young salmon with the same problem.

SNAPPER: A junior bluefish with a senior appetite.

SPOTTED BASS: A bass only seen in certain spots.

SPOON: A bright, metallic lure used to attract the fish. Spoons take their name from the way they were supposed to have originated. Legend has it that a fisherman once went out with potato salad for lunch. While eating the junk, he dropped his spoon overboard. As it sank, a passing fish with an appetite for potato salad took a bite at it. The fish ate the potato salad and died of ptomaine poisoning. This led to the further use of spoons to lure fish. But modern nimrods invariably forget to add potato salad to their spoons. As a result, they catch nothing at all.

SURF FISHING: The practice of traveling to a nearby ocean and tossing bait into the surf for hours on end. An expert surf fisherman can stand motionless for five hours without hating himself in the morning. Amateurs must practice for at least two seasons before becoming such damned fools.

TACKLE: Assorted junk used to fill a tackle box.

TACKLE BOX: (See Tackle)

TAILING: Deceptive habit of certain fish who turn upside down to explore bottoms of shallow pools. When fish waves tail on surface, fisherman casts bait in direction of the disturbance. This leads to occasional hooking of trout by tail, sometimes called Lucky Strike among cigarette smoking anglers.

TROLLING: The art of dangling a line off the rear end of a slow moving boat to attract fish toward bait. Good trollers are experts at getting nowhere and taking their time about it. Trolling is recommended for all sportsmen who enjoy boat rides, gentle breezes and plenty of sunshine. Sportsmen who like to catch fish had better try other methods.

VIRGINIA HOOK: An old friend of my wife, included here because a hook was named after her.

WADER: Long rubber boots for taking walks in the water. For longer, deeper walks, use longer, deeper waders.

WAHOO: A sensible fish with a very crazy name.

YELLOW PERCH: A very cowardly perch.

ZERO: What most nimrods catch.

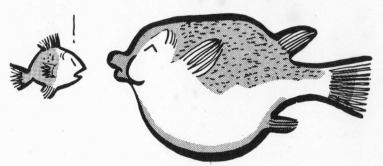

THE BLOWFISH

If I live to be a hundred
I will never figure out,
What the stupid little blowfish
Has to blow about!